Tipping Sacred Cows

Tipping Sacred Cows

Kick the Bad Work Habits That Masquerade as Virtues

Jake Breeden

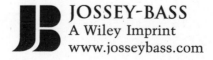

JOSSEY-BASS
A Wiley Imprint
www.josseybass.com

Cover design by Adrian Morgan
Cover image: © Thinkstock (RF)

Copyright © 2013 by John Wiley & Sons, Inc. All rights reserved.

Published by Jossey-Bass
A Wiley Imprint
One Montgomery Street, Suite 1200, San Francisco, CA 94104-4594—www.josseybass.com

Jossey-Bass books and products are available through most bookstores. To contact Jossey-Bass directly call our Customer Care Department within the U.S. at 800-956-7739, outside the U.S. at 317-572-3986, or fax 317-572-4002.

Wiley publishes in a variety of print and electronic formats and by print-on-demand. Some material included with standard print versions of this book may not be included in e-books or in print-on-demand. If this book refers to media such as a CD or DVD that is not included in the version you purchased, you may download this material at http://booksupport.wiley.com. For more information about Wiley products, visit www.wiley.com.

Library of Congress Cataloging-in-Publication Data

Breeden, Jake, 1972–
  Tipping sacred cows: kick the bad work habits that masquerade as virtues / Jake Breeden.—First edition.
      pages cm
  Includes bibliographical references and index.
  ISBN 978-1-118-34591-7 (cloth); ISBN 978-1-118-53190-7 (ebk.);
ISBN 978-1-118-43192-4 (ebk.); ISBN 978-1-118-43191-7 (ebk.)
  1. Organizational effectiveness. 2. Management—Psychological aspects. 3. Performance. I. Title.
  HD58.9.B734 2013
  650.1—dc23
                                                                                        2012041895

Printed in the United States of America
FIRST EDITION
HB Printing   10 9 8 7 6 5 4 3 2 1

Contents

To Emily, Clara, and Margaret.

Tipping Sacred Cows

1

Meet Your Sacred Cows

I get paid to do my two favorite things: travel and teach. I love my work. Over the past ten years I've been to twenty-seven countries, working with some really smart, successful leaders at exciting companies. But there's something I love even more than my job — Emily, Clara, and Margaret, my three daughters.

I go into withdrawal if it's been too long since I've seen them. And there's one absolutely sacrosanct rule for me: never miss a birthday. Despite the intensity of my international travel, I made it through my oldest daughter Emily's first twelve years, my middle daughter Clara's first nine years, and my youngest daughter Margaret's first five years without ever missing a birthday, a perfect twenty-six for twenty-six. And then came Clara's tenth birthday.

I had to teach a two-week leadership development program in Dubai. I hated it, but I decided teaching the program and missing Clara's birthday was the only responsible thing to do. I sat down with her to discuss what I could do to make amends, knowing this was a negotiation I was bound to lose. I showed up with a heart full of guilt, ready to do whatever it took to placate my middle child. "Clara, I'm going to be out of the country for your birthday," I said.

"My double-digit birthday?" she asked.

"Yes," I swallowed. "That one."

And then came the sobs. I hugged her. "Daddy?" she asked through muffled tears. "Will you do anything I ask you to, to make up for missing my double-digit birthday?"

I hesitated before asking a dangerous question: "What do you want?"

"Daddy," she said, drying her big blue eyes as she pulled away from me. "I want you to promise me that you'll miss Emily's thirteenth birthday."

I had expected to be looking into the price of Justin Bieber tickets. I was ready to give Clara something special, not take away something special from her sister.

Clara said I should miss Emily's birthday "because it's fair." I was missing a special birthday for her, and I needed to make up for that by missing a special birthday for Emily. The way to make amends was to even the score.

Unwilling to start an endless chain reaction of missed birthdays, I took Clara to a theme park—one of her favorite and my least favorite things to do. When I stepped off the roller coaster quivering with nausea, Clara finally felt the score was even. Someone had to pay, and that someone was me.

None of us wants to be treated unfairly. From our earliest days, we, like Clara, have a sense that life should be fair and we protest or seethe when it's not. To even the scales, we demand something for ourselves. Failing that, we deny something for others. To be sure, fairness is a virtue, but when it's a virtue that trumps reason, it can backfire.

As it turns out, Clara's response was not unlike the typical responses of well-meaning adults. When they waste precious emotional energy fretting over relative office size, bonus packages, or mentions at the annual meeting, or when they demand that a junior employee go through the same trivial grunt work and dreadful schedule that they did, even if there's a better way, leaders make the same mistake as Clara. Sometimes worrying about who gets more than their fair share is a lot like tearfully asking your father to miss your sister's birthday.

Fairness is only one of several leadership virtues whose pursuit can reap unintended, injurious consequences. The truth is that many workplace values that seem beyond reproach actually do hidden damage. These are values that on the one hand give us life and direction, and on the other hand can steal our energy, effectiveness, and success. Like rocks in a river channel, these unexamined values can get in our way, impede our efforts, and even capsize us. Some leaders, however, become fully aware and steadily mindful of the downsides of their and their companies' most cherished and unquestioned virtues, and, in the process, renew their spirits, get more done, and enjoy more success.

Unexamined Virtues at Work

No detail escaped Julian Fletcher's watchful eye. As the COO of a small but growing consulting firm, he counted every penny, balanced every budget, and demanded that his employees operate with the same ruthless efficiency. And though Julian was successful in his role, he was often frustrated by the cavalier attitude of his boss, the CEO. When the CEO was recruited away to run a larger firm, Julian was promoted to the top position, and without wasting a second, he eagerly set out to tighten the ship.

First, he eliminated several client entertainment events at expensive restaurants. Next, he ended the firm's policy of giving away free consulting to prospective clients. Then, he slashed the firm's liberal expense policy and stopped the practice of wooing new recruits with large bonuses.

At first, Julian's results were impressive. The company's costs dropped, which in turn made profits rise. But over the next several months, signs of damage emerged. Clients and employees began to disengage. A few workers jumped ship to other companies. No new clients signed on, deals from existing clients began to dry up, and the flow of talented new hires ceased. By the end of Julian's first year, profits began to sink.

In an act of near mutiny, a few of the firm's employees reached out to the former CEO, begging her to come back and offer Julian advice.

Out of loyalty to her former company and colleagues, she agreed. And out of desperation, Julian reluctantly acquiesced to meet with his former boss.

"Julian," she said, "when you took over after I left, the company was growing rapidly in spite of some obvious inefficiencies. You acted with the best of intentions as you tried to eliminate some of the waste you saw. But in the process of cutting the loss, you've also destroyed the growth. Now, the firm has gone from growing inefficiently to shrinking efficiently."

Julian's belief in efficiency was his sacred cow—a virtue he revered without question—and with good reason: it is a core business value, and he fostered it with zeal. Leaders like Julian often end up baffled. The very virtues that helped them succeed earlier in their career betray them as they move up the ladder. It's smart to rely on your core beliefs at work. But thriving in the corporate world, in any role, requires the ability to recognize, on a personal level, when your greatest assets turn into career-limiting liabilities. On the organizational level, successful leadership requires being able to see when unexamined virtues have actually become, or are masking, unsuspected vices.

My own understanding of the unintended consequences of conventional workplace wisdom is grounded in my experience working with executives all over the world and informed by surprising research in psychology and economics on how human nature, social norms, and corporate culture can all pull us toward the territory of unexamined virtues. A growing body of research indicates these supposed virtues can wreak havoc on the careers of leaders and the results of organizations. Experiments by economists in The Netherlands have demonstrated the dark side of fairness;[1] a French-Canadian psychology professor discovered how passion for work can become an unhealthy obsession;[2] and a political science professor researching the marksmanship of female marines showed how aiming for excellence can backfire.[3]

Researchers aren't the only ones who challenge convention. Successful business leaders increasingly reject sacred cows at work. The insights and solutions I offer here are informed by my experience with executives all over the world, helping them discover and learn to avoid some of the most common, destructive, and invisible ways that business virtues and values backfire. Because in the world of work, when virtue backfires, it can lower performance, waste time and energy, damage morale and retention, and ruin careers.

The Peril of Sacred Cows

My teaching travels have taken me throughout India, to Mumbai, Delhi, Bangalore, Ahmedabad, Calcutta, and elsewhere. Between leadership trainings, I've vacationed on the stunning beaches of the Indian resort town Goa. The first literary reference to Goa from the *Mahabharata* refers to the city as Gomanta, which means "region of cows."[4] "Go" means cow in Sanskrit, the primary liturgical language of Hinduism. It's no surprise, then, that cows are plentiful in Goa.

Although I was warned about the cows beforehand, it still shocked me to see them milling slowly down busy streets, lovingly adorned in handmade necklaces and bright orange strings of marigolds. They roam leisurely until they are brought back to their homes at the end of each day to rest and provide for families. These cows, givers of milk, are literally sacred objects of sincere reverence. "Sacred cow" is a Western figure of speech that takes its cue from the literal holy cows of India. It's an idea, custom, or institution that has real virtue, but that we hold beyond question or criticism — often unreasonably so. In the workplace, the danger of sacred cows is that in not approaching them with a healthy dose of mindfulness, we become blind to the ways these virtues sometimes hurt us. We fail to learn from our mistakes, and we stay stuck. And sometimes we stray badly off course.

Powerful, often invisible behavioral, social, and cultural forces can cause leaders to espouse the infallible importance of unexamined virtues in their ascent to success. One of the mightiest of those forces is the advice passed down from successful leaders, who attribute their success to such virtues. Ask leaders what gave rise to their wins and they might point to their high standards. But Clay Christensen's research, starting with *The Innovator's Dilemma*, shows that sometimes "good enough" is better than excellent.[5] Other leaders celebrate collaborating with others effectively, but Morten Hansen, the U.C. Berkeley business professor who literally wrote the book on collaboration (called *Collaboration*), uses rigorous research to show that "collaboration can just as easily undermine performance."[6] Hansen's tougher examination of success reveals the occasional but critical role of less obvious and celebrated factors like hunkering down to take care of your own work and being open and ready to act on good luck.

Senior executives with a short attention span who constantly scan for new stimuli and boldly bet their careers on new opportunities may accomplish great things in part because of their *lack* of focus and follow through. But rather than advise their people to behave in this way, they often advocate unrelenting focus and concentration on the task at hand. I don't suggest the executives mean to mislead. Just as a bird isn't an ornithologist, a leader isn't a behavioral scientist. The best leaders don't sit back and study their success — they're too busy achieving it.

When Stephen Jay Gould died in 2002, *American Scientist* remembered him as "an extraordinary figure in paleontology and evolutionary biology ... [who] initiated and shaped some of the most heated and productive debates of the second half of the 20th century."[7] Gould attacked human chauvinism, the tendency to view evolution as a long march from the simple to the complex, leading up to humanity as the apex of evolution. Gould called bullshit on this view and used a massive body of statistical evidence to question the prevailing notion that evolution is a systematic march of progress. Instead, he showed it's more of a random, "drunkard's walk." Questioning the march of evolution toward complexity was the modern-day equivalent of Galileo suggesting that the sun doesn't revolve around the earth. Galileo used data to show we're not the center of the world, and Gould used data to show we're not the point of evolution. Gould was a great tipper of sacred cows and I admire his courage and hard work to support his points of view with evidence. My favorite Gould quotation, from his book *Full House: The Spread of Excellence from Plato to Darwin*, nicely sums up one of the key themes of *Tipping Sacred Cows*: "The most erroneous stories are those we think we know best — and therefore never scrutinize or question."[8]

Think about the stories you know best. There's one story I imagine you know especially well: the story of how you got where you are. And you've probably shared some of the lessons of your stories with others, as teaching is a natural act of leadership. We tell ourselves — and each other — stories that explain our own progress through life so often that the lessons of those stories become our truth. I think it's time to scrutinize and question those stories.

In addition to the well-meaning stories we tell ourselves, another trusted source pushes us to overvalue virtues like fairness — our brains. As reported in "The Sunny Side of Fairness," an article from the April, 2008 *Psychological Science*, our brain's reward circuitry is activated when we receive an offer we perceive to be fair.[9] And scholars have shown how mirror neurons in the brain encourage primates, including us humans, to feel what others feel.[10] We're social animals programmed at a deep level to empathize, help each other, and generally ensure things end up fair. Helping others is indeed a real virtue reflecting a real human need. But not everyone wants what we want, and our brain can too easily be fooled. If you yearn for a little more attention and acclaim at work, your neural reward circuitry lights up when you give someone else attention and acclaim — even if the other person would prefer to be left alone. Your brain's reward circuitry can't peer into someone else's brain. So we can confuse sameness with fairness and give others the rewards we seek. Or worse, we may even arbitrarily sabotage others to bring them down to our level, because it feels better for us to maintain a personal sense of justice.

Our own internal drives extend beyond fairness. We have, for example, a powerful, natural urge to finish tasks once we start them. Even when it might be wiser to abandon work, we have an urge to push through to completion. This phenomenon was established in a series of studies decades ago: nearly 100 percent of those tested in studies in the 1930s, '40s, and '50s demonstrated a strong desire to return to interrupted tasks such as completing a puzzle.[11] Our natural desire to finish a task we start helps us see things through to the end, but it hurts our ability to recognize the times when the smartest decision is to quit.

But it's not just the advice of well-intended leaders or the urges of our well-intended brains that cause us to fall into the trap of blindly following seemingly virtuous traits. The silent pull of our organization's culture also convinces smart leaders to blindly obey sacred cows. For example, when a company claims it values excellence in everything, the culture can inhibit exploration and quick prototyping. Or, if it's not safe to show and share half-baked ideas, the company misses out on some really great fully baked new ones. On the other hand, cultures that lionize creativity may shift a leader's focus away from pragmatic innovation toward newness for the sake of newness, or for the sake of ego and attention. And finally, a culture that idolizes balance may pull leaders to make bland compromises instead of standing for distinctive, meaningful work.

Let me be clear. I would *never* suggest that devout Hindus consider how tasty their beloved cows might be if they cooked and ate them. Similarly I don't suggest we kill conventional wisdom. The point of this book isn't to slaughter sacred cows. The point is to save them, and we do that by tipping them over and examining them. By understanding when and how to use our most heartfelt beliefs we can avoid their nasty unintended consequences. Julian Fletcher shouldn't stop being efficient — he needs to start being more sophisticated. He needs to raise his game so he understands how efficiency can harmonize with other complementary leadership traits he needs to nourish.

When leaders embrace beliefs without understanding and managing the potential side effects, the beliefs become sacred cows and get in the way. When leaders shut off their brains and blindly follow the bromides of conventional wisdom they set off a string of unintended consequences. I write this book because I have seen the same heartbreaking story play out too many times. Well-intended leaders, driven by deeply held beliefs, try to do the right thing — but the right thing backfires.

Business virtues help you most when they are used on purpose, not out of habit. With mindfulness and self-awareness, leaders can filter through advice and conventional wisdom to act purposefully. When you thoughtfully embrace a virtue, it is your friend. But when you do so out of habit, fear, or compliance you waste energy and risk losing your way. By resisting the quiet, consistent undertow of convention, you honor the wisdom of business virtues and you flourish as a leader. But when you unthinkingly accept your sacred cows, you pay a tax. The tax can come in many forms: wasted energy, frustration, poor performance, and burnout. But the worst part of the sacred cow tax is that you don't even know you're paying it.

Solving the Virtue Problem

Jealousy, selfishness, and greed are demons that some leaders grapple with, and there are many places to look for help if these are your issues. But I find virtue that is secretly harmful to be a much more interesting problem than obvious vice. I'm driven to help well-meaning leaders discover problems they don't know they have, not to help lazy leaders work on the issues they've been willfully accepting for years. When leaders work to play cynical survival games to lie low and make it through to retirement without getting laid off, I feel no urge to help them. I shed no tears for the demise of lazy, cynical, selfish leaders afraid to lead. But I'm galvanized when I see someone held back *because* of their good intentions. I'm most interested in helping leaders who fail because they did something they felt good about, not because they did something that felt wrong.

Steve, the head of an accounting department at a hospital, can't break his collaboration habit. His boss needs him to take the risk to provide a quick opinion in a senior off-site meeting, but Steve feels compelled to return to work and seek the input of his team before making a recommendation. His belief in collaboration prevents him from stepping up and giving his own point of view on the fly. He blindly follows the path of collaboration to inaction, makes a decision too slowly, and misses the opportunity to lead.

The real shame is that Steve likely doesn't see the flaw in his ways and thus hasn't learned anything. Ask him what happened, and he'll tell you his boss doesn't value collaboration highly enough. I asked Steve to consider another possibility: maybe he believed in collaboration so much because it feels good—and, in this case, because it kept him from having to stick his neck out and offer his own point of view. Sometimes, without realizing it, we use our most treasured values as an excuse to avoid the discomfort of actually leading. I believe Steve has good judgment and is capable of making quick decisions. But his belief in collaboration blocks him from setting free his latent abilities and allowing them to shine.

Good intentions that turn into bad decisions are among the most interesting—and insidious and frustrating—problems I see in workplaces today. It's devastating to see a man plateau at work because he has been told to be collaborative and now he's collaborating so much it's choking him. Or a woman who has been encouraged to maintain the highest standards struggle, unable to see how her drive to be excellent in all things causes her superiors to view her as "stuck in the weeds" and therefore not ready for promotion. Leaders need the wherewithal to ask forbidden questions: Why should I collaborate? Is passion healthy? Does everything I do need my best effort? Should I prepare less? Should I care less? Leaders need to be wise to the seductive power of unquestioned orthodoxies.

Why are sacred cows so attractive and why do they exist? When do they help and when do they hurt? There isn't a single answer to any of these questions. Various virtues operate differently from one another, and they become sacred cows in individual, specific ways. The nature of excellence, for example, is completely different from that of fairness, which in turn is completely different from collaboration. Each of these virtues-turned-sacred-cows emerges from a particular mix of culture and cognition. In this book, I analyze the seven most destructive sacred cows with the intention of building up your awareness of them. I'll rely on stories from the real world of business and from current academic research.

The real world launches products, plans budgets, designs systems, and makes tradeoffs. The real world can be a productive place, except that, unexamined, the real world tends to keep replaying the same corporate comedies and tragedies over and over. Here's where the academy comes in. Researchers at universities examine the real world and build theories that explain why things happen as they do. We, the actors in these recurring dramas, use the theories to gain needed insight into and awareness about ourselves and our world. Ideally, we achieve a measure of enlightenment and stop making the same mistakes. And, in this way, the real world gets smarter. But theory needs to be grounded. Like the real world, theory isn't flawless, and too often it glides above reality, disconnected from the world it describes. Insights from theories can lose context and become too abstract to be useful.

My intellectual training ground, Duke Corporate Education (Duke CE), exists to help the real world have its theoretical cake and eat it too. Although Duke University's basketball team, medical school and other programs are each highly ranked, only its custom executive education service—Duke CE—has been ranked number one in the world every year over a ten-year period, from 2003 to 2012 (by the *Financial Times* of London and *BusinessWeek*). I spent my thirties working for and with Duke CE, living at the crossroads of two worlds: the academic world of ideas and the practical world of action. This book lives at that intersection.

Duke CE has been successful because the people there help their clients resist both the cynical tug of a hopelessly real world mired in its recurring dramas *and* the false promise of an escape to idealistically pure theory. The people at Duke CE know that the work that matters is real enough to be practical right away and insightful enough to be of long-lasting value. Overcoming the sacred cows holding you back at work requires new, research-based theories and the pragmatic examples of real-world leadership.

Find Your Hidden Beliefs

An unexamined reverence for sacred cows is a wide-ranging, universal phenomenon. But in order to help you achieve real performance improvement, we need to get specific. The seven business virtues that can turn into the most powerful, hidden, and damaging sacred cows are: balance, collaboration, creativity, excellence, fairness, passion, and preparation.

In their manifestation as sacred cows, these seven qualities show up in workplaces around the world, in every industry, and at every level of leadership, and they are rarely questioned. Each has a well-deserved reputation for being good and virtuous. But that reputation lulls leaders into a complacency that can blind them to the harsh effects these seven can have when left unexamined. I focus on these seven because they are the most frequently advocated, widely beloved, and least frequently questioned orthodoxies at work.

Take a look at the symptoms of each of the seven sacred cows as I describe them below, and do a little self-screening to diagnose your biggest backfire. You'll likely recognize yourself or someone else in one or more of them. To be sure, the complete absence of any of these virtues would be a tremendous problem for any leader. The trick is in cultivating an awareness of when and how they function well, when and how they backfire, and how to recalibrate them so that they're helping and not hurting.

Balance

In modern life and in the modern workplace, balance is a hallowed virtue. Balance operates through a constant stream of choices. In an effort to be balanced, leaders make choices to be and do many different things. They may choose to be both strong parents and strong managers. They may choose to focus on both short-term results and long-term strategy, or to be both detail oriented and visionary. All of these choices can too easily drift toward the middle in a cowardly compromise of nothingness. Balance backfires when it moves from being about bold, sometimes tough, choices to being about bland compromises. If a leader, in striving for balance, is mediocre at everything (or engenders mediocrity in her employees), then balance has backfired.

Balance is valuable. Avoiding extremes and embracing moderation is often wise. Similarly, considering both sides of an argument before acting serves us well. The Founding Fathers separated powers in the

American government, creating a system of checks and balances that would prevent any one individual or group from seizing all control. And anyone who has tried to work too many eighty-hour weeks or tried to subsist on a diet of coffee and donuts alone knows that balance is a virtue. Balance is particularly helpful at times of transition, when first-time managers seek to complement their technical skills with softer leadership skills. When an accountant makes partner, she may need to balance her accounting skills with the ability to win business and lead teams. When a highly skilled programmer is asked to lead a team of other programmers, he may need to learn new social, team-building, and administrative skills to augment his technical acumen.

But when "balance" is misconstrued to mean constant compromise, several unfortunate things happen. You can't outsmart a dilemma by avoiding it in the name of balance. If you try to balance work and life by doing everything at once you'll do everything poorly. Bold leaders must make tough choices. And when we as leaders move from doing one thing well to many things poorly, our organizations suffer. Leaders who hide behind balance as an excuse to avoid taking a stand for an unpopular position do themselves and their companies a disservice. In short, when balance encourages us to say yes to everything all at once, we end up saying no to leadership.

I call this dysfunctional pursuit of balance *bland balance*. It leads us to compromise in the face of dilemmas, make unnecessary trade-offs in an attempt to seek safety, divide our attention, delay or duck necessary decisions, and handle uncertainty poorly.

Its remedy is *bold balance*. Bold balance at work rejects compromise as a default, work-life balance as a constant, mastery of all things as an expectation, holding unpopular positions as a taboo, and saying yes to all things as wisdom. You can achieve bold balance when you respect the model of moderation and balanced scales but also hold up other conceptions of balance as equally valid. The ebb and flow of waves and the tides help maintain a balanced ecosystem and avoid extremes such as flooding—but the ocean itself is anything but safe and bland. And four (sometimes extreme) seasons point to a continuing and complex balance among many natural cycles. Balance is a dynamic process that requires your constant attention and awareness.

Collaboration

When I talk about "collaboration" in the context of this book, I mean working together with people in your organization. Collaboration becomes a sacred cow when it is automatic. It's a strong part of good leadership, and can be part of an effective work style, when it is accountable. *Automatic collaboration* means working together by default instead of making the purposeful, conscious choice to do so. The default state of working should be working alone; leaders should collaborate only when they must. Depending on your role, that may mean a significant part of your job requires collaboration. But ask yourself the question: does this work really need more than me? Or am I simply engaging in automatic collaboration?

When leaders do collaborate, it must be accountable, not automatic. Accountable collaboration means everyone has a clear understanding of the mission of the team, and the goal of the team is to achieve its mission and disband. When collaboration is accountable, everyone knows everyone else's responsibility, and they aren't afraid to point out when the ball is dropped.

Great advances have been achieved through working together. As American cultural anthropologist Margaret Mead reportedly said, "Never doubt that a small group of thoughtful, committed citizens can change the world. Indeed, it is the only thing that ever has." Humans must work together to solve difficult problems. Research shows the power of teams. When we strive for greater diversity in teams by crossing national or continental cultures, or by mixing disciplines and demographics, civilized enlightenment and new insights arise. When previously unsolvable problems find solutions through crowdsourcing, collaboration makes miracles. When problems are more fully understood, when logic is rigorously tested, or when richer ideas are generated, working in teams makes companies perform better.

But when working together has become an unexamined cultural norm, it can cause big problems:

- Leaders often peg a worker who performs independent tasks apart from a team as antisocial.
- A culture of learned helplessness can arise, causing, for example, a product manager to fear being decisive about a new feature without exhaustively interviewing teammates and coming to a consensus. Naturally, innovation suffers.
- Workgroups can grow too big and lose their focus, their roles and responsibilities morphing into ambiguity, lack of accountability, and time wasted.
- Team structures can engender corporate dysfunction when "underlap" creeps into projects, with team members assuming someone else will get the task done.
- Working with others is sometimes a blast, sometimes a must, and sometimes a waste. Accountable collaboration respects teamwork as a tool you can use when a situation demands it. In small groups, when you distinguish roles and outline rules of engagement, your team can be greater than the sum of its parts. Collaboration works when you and your team complement each other and are all accountable for your own contribution. Knowing the when and how of working collaboratively multiplies your effectiveness. This means avoiding collaboration as a default.

Creativity

Creativity involves bringing something new into the world. It's an enticing quality—it can be fun and exciting to exercise creativity, and creative breakthroughs can make a real difference to companies or whole industries. But often an old idea will do just fine. If not, then combining two existing ideas to make a new combination will usually suffice. If you've carefully studied the past, looking without shame to borrow, modify, or recycle an existing idea, then you're using *useful creativity* —being creative enough to be effective within the context of the enterprise at hand.

But too often creativity backfires because of a leader's need to add her own ideas. This is *narcissistic creativity*. Adopting someone else's best practice doesn't give you the same sense of pride and accomplishment as generating a new best practice. Creating a needless innovation feels better to the innovator than does creating nothing at all. In such cases, creativity has stopped being a tool used in service of larger goals, and has become the very personal source of a leader's narcissistic needs.

Sure, the world needs creators. Without new designs, new products and new business models, leaders risk losing out to more innovative competitors and economies risk decline. Moreover, creativity often makes life better. It drives commerce, with old ideas giving way to new— horses to cars, telegraphs to radios, and dial-up to Wi-Fi.

Nurses who come up with creative ways to improve patient intake demonstrate the emergent leadership and creative problem solving that save lives. Customer service representatives who think of creative ways to better serve customers add meaningful value to their companies. CEOs who see flagging business models and rally teams to come up with new and better ways to structure deals help ensure the value of shareholder equity.

But too often we overvalue creativity. As part of her doctoral research completed at the University of North Carolina, Tina Juillerat shows that despite the enthusiastic, well-meaning quest for creativity at the workplace, it's not clear that more creative ideas lead to more innovation. In fact, her studies show that the more novel an idea, the less likely it is to become part of a value-generating innovation.[12]

The urge to feel the creative spark can cause us to feel compelled to leave our mark on an organization. But too often the urge to produce creative work springs from the leader's own drive to leave a legacy instead of meeting a real business need. Leaders who invent something new— to meet their internal needs for ego gratification— when something old will do only yield destruction, waste, and dysfunction.

Useful creativity delivers value, not just novelty.

Excellence

Excellence means high quality; our pursuit of it backfires when our high standards choke progress. This typically happens when we are focused on excellence in the *process* rather than excellence in the *outcome*. When our excellence muscle is exercised to ensure that every step of a process is flawless, we may worry too much; we may not take enough steps, or the right ones; and we may lose sight of the bigger picture. Instead of holding our process to such a high standard, there are times when we need only focus on aiming for excellence in a final outcome. In these instances it's tolerance for quick failures, followed by constant learning and tweaking, that are most likely to lead us to the best possible result.

Hearing Beethoven's sonatas or seeing Michelangelo's Sistine Chapel ceiling expand our ideas of what is possible and enriches our imaginations. We follow athletes who dazzle us with win after win and record after record, and delight in the capabilities of human physical effort. We know good work when we see it, and we award respect to those who make excellence a habit and wow us with consistent quality.

A salesperson who respects a customer enough to know a product cold, listen well, understand a customer's needs, and surpass expectations with follow-through every time deserves praise. A pharmacist who triple-checks correct dosages prevents medical emergencies. A quality assurance engineer who serves as the last line of defense prior to a product launch and painstakingly tests all new features in each type of web browser protects against technology failures.

So some say good enough is for wimps, losers, and copouts. But we set a trap for ourselves when we expect excellence in everything, when excellence becomes a standard that's ongoing and omnipresent. Regardless of how great a leader's accomplishments are, there is always another ladder to climb. Excellence is the drug of choice for the ambitious perfectionist, and it can lead to exhaustion and ruin. High standards are wasted on activities of low importance because leaders can't give themselves a break. Some leaders obsess over every mistake, even the ones that don't matter. Sure, the sales plan needs to be directionally correct. But wouldn't it be better to spend more time selling and less time polishing the plan? Sure, you need to have the buy-in of your executive team, but wouldn't they rather you just get started instead of wasting time covering your ass with approvals?

When excellence is worshipped, it becomes a goal in and of itself, disconnected from larger goals. If you suspect excellence backfires for you, reflect on the connection between your self-esteem and your work. Do you need to cut that cord? Can you use rough drafts and prototypes to start, learn, and improve quickly? To avoid the side effects of excellence, you'll need to differentiate between what *can* be done in the name of excellence and what *should* be done in the name of progress.

Fairness

When I examine "fairness" as a virtue or sacred cow, I'm talking about the treatment we give to others and receive from others at work. Fairness backfires when some of our noblest instincts force us to ensure equitable outcomes rather than equitable processes (in this way it's a mirror image of excellence, which is healthy when focused on outcomes and goes off the rails when focused on process). A leader's job is to make sure everyone — including herself — has a fair chance. Fairness can easily backfire as the line between a fair chance and a seemingly fair result is often blurred. After all, it's much easier to look at and discuss the fairness of the result than it is to ensure a fair process. The result is often objective and tangible — office size, bonus, awards, promotions — whereas the process is a squishy mess of dozens of little decisions.

The urge to be treated fairly and to treat others fairly comes from two very strong places: nature and nurture. Scientists have shown how our neurochemistry encourages us to find a fair outcome so we can activate our brain's reward network. And we are taught fairness as children, and encouraged as adults to be fair. If people didn't value fairness, what kind of world would we have? Laws and customs based on the principle of fairness protect fundamental rights and ensure that guilty parties pay for their wrongdoing.

But in the world of work, this strong tug toward fairness can lead to some nasty unintended consequences:

- Sometimes leaders avoid making exceptions for even exceptional performance, afraid of feeling unfair or being accused of unfairness. Think of the boss who sent his best employee to a training trip in Switzerland last year. This year he only has the budget to send one of his employees to a training trip in Costa Rica, but he's not willing to send his best employee again because it doesn't feel fair.
- Fairness also backfires when leaders keep score, counting exactly what someone else was given. In the process, they burn precious emotional and intellectual energy in the unproductive game of making sure everyone gets his or her fair share.
- Most troubling is the research that shows that people who feel they have been unfairly treated are more likely to bend the rules. One disturbing study showed that some business school students who felt their effort wasn't appropriately rewarded with high grades were more likely to cheat on an exam.[13]
- To honor fairness in process and not necessarily in results, you need the courage to treat people differently, make appropriate exceptions, and dole out punishments when needed. As a leader, you need to be able to discriminate between what you want or need and what someone else wants or needs. You'll need to avoid the wasted energy of deciding whether you got your fair share at work, and to train yourself to focus your fire on beating the competition instead of your colleagues. And, importantly, learn to recognize the times when you use fairness as an excuse to make decisions you'll later regret.

Passion

"Passion," for our purposes, means the quality of caring deeply about your work. It's a good and healthy thing when a passion for work is in harmony with other parts of your life. If caring about one part of your work makes you better at some other aspect of the job, then it is a healthy, *harmonious passion*. But passion backfires when it becomes obsessive. *Obsessive passion* crowds out other aspects of your life and your work, causing you to ruminate on one thing at the expense of others.

We can see the passion of our most successful leaders. Their long hours, sweat, and enthusiasm are readily observable, and it's natural for us to want to emulate that energy. But less visible traits like judgment, emotional maturity, and sophistication often lie beneath the surface of passion. When passion is healthy, it's not an independent force, but a part of a diverse set of traits. Workers fueled by harmonious passion are not less driven than their obsessive colleagues. Instead, they are better supported, because they have invested in building a diverse set of long-term relationships and interests. Good passion is in harmony with other aspects of a leader's life.

Bad passion crowds out everything else; it is characterized by obsessive attitude and compulsive action. Obsessive passion leads to wild swings from huge enthusiasm at the start of a project to disappointment and regret when delays, challenges, or changes arise. It's worth remembering that high-octane fuel helps cars run faster because, counterintuitively, it burns more slowly. If you're fueled by the cheap stuff that flames out fast you'll need to learn to avoid burnout by shutting down more frequently, more completely, and with greater effect.

Preparation

By "preparation," I mean getting yourself ready to do work. Sometimes the preparation and the work happen at nearly the same time, which can be both healthy and productive. Too much *backstage preparation* isn't helpful. It can delay work without improving the product: hiding out and reading is not helpful preparation; polishing slides is not as helpful as starting the meeting and learning in real time. *Onstage preparation* happens when you're learning as you're doing. It's the exhilarating, powerful process of making yourself vulnerable to be persuaded and changed, even as you're attempting to persuade. Leaders who prepare onstage have the guts to admit to themselves and others that they are always a work in progress. And through this commitment, these leaders make so much more progress than if they viewed preparation as separate from the work. Preparation backstage happens alone, without the benefit of real-time feedback. Backstage preparation backfires because it slows down our development and because it too often leads us to fall in love with a script we've worked hard to prepare, at the expense of being flexible and always willing to learn more about the material.

Preparation is one of the most widely celebrated virtues: measure and prep the ingredients before cooking a meal; stretch before a run; and do your "homework" before a job interview or a client meeting. By preparing ahead of time, you give yourself a significant advantage. You build your capabilities, practice the fundamentals, and come off the blocks equipped for success. From the Boy Scout motto—"Be Prepared"—to SAT prep classes, we are taught from an early age that good results go to those who are ready.

When we learn and expand our skills without falling in love with our work, preparation is a good thing. And preparation *is* critical for the moments when leaders truly need to develop their expertise to reduce the risk of a critical failure. But preparation can backfire in unexpected ways. Professors who sought to test the effect of preparation on test performance were surprised to learn that requiring homework actually reduced students' exam scores in an operations management class. In their study, students in "Treatment A" were in a section of a class that had to complete problem sets as part of their grade, while "Treatment B" students were in a different section of the same class that had no homework assignments. In the words of the paper's authors, "Contrary to our expectations, students given Treatment A had a lower overall exam mean than did the Treatment B students." Expending too much energy in homework, it seemed, had sapped the students' ability to concentrate on the exam.[14]

In the workplace, preparation can backfire by causing you to fall in love with your work to the point that you defend what you should change. It backfires when your work becomes your baby. And sometimes, preparation is merely an excuse not to take action.

Leaders who master onstage preparation thrive on feedback and improvisation. They avoid overpreparing things that don't matter, and thus funnel their time and energy wisely. When you jettison such old mental models of preparation as studying for tests and move toward viewing all work performance as an opportunity to deepen your skills and prepare for the next stages of work, you free yourself up to use time more effectively and accelerate your skill building and your learning.

Train Your Cow, Train Yourself

Julian, the CEO of the small consulting firm who struggled in his first year at the top, had spent his entire life learning the lesson that strategy is often overrated. Execution is everything, thought Julian. But when his former boss stepped in to offer a new perspective, Julian learned a new lesson and began charting a new course.

"As you know," he told his entire staff at a special company meeting, "I like to run a tight ship. But the only reason you tighten up the ship is so she'll sail faster. Now that we've tightened things up around here, I need your help in picking up our speed so we can grow more rapidly than ever. But this time, we'll grow smartly."

He called his new plan "Growth, Version 2," but it was really "Julian, Version 2." He put together several two-week teams charged with making concrete suggestions on smart ways to bring back some of the fun and rewards that had driven growth at the firm. After two weeks, the groups were disbanded as planned. Although Julian maintained his belief in the power of efficient implementation, he grew as a leader by listening to his people. He took the best recommendations from his people and put some of the positive energy back into the company, all while running a tighter ship. The growth rate returned, but this time without the waste.

In India, drivers sometimes have to work hard to make their way around the cows that roam the crowded streets. Figurative sacred cows—the kind that we find in the workplace—may be harder to see, but once discovered they can be avoided. In each of the chapters ahead, I share real-world stories, academic research, and solutions to help you train yourself to avoid allowing workplace virtues—and your own personal strengths and preferences — to turn into sacred cows. You may recognize yourself or someone you work with in some of the stories of the dark side of workplace virtues. The research will help you understand more deeply how and why the sacred cows came to be so powerful and, in some cases, so powerfully destructive. Each chapter has solutions designed to help you train yourself to avoid the waste that comes from the unintended consequences of unexamined conventional wisdom. By finally recognizing and avoiding the power and peril of sacred cows at work, leaders can find a clear path between their best intentions and the success they deserve.

If you'd like a custom report to help you focus your attention on the chapters that relate most to your own biggest sacred cows at work, visit my website and take the free, five-minute assessment: http://www .breedenideas.com.

2

Bland Bold Balance

Ann loved her job. She worked at a large bank as a philanthropic adviser to high-net-worth individuals, and her job demanded she stay sharp at finance, philanthropy, and cultivating strong relationships. Her clients were typically at the end of their careers and came to Ann with two goals: help me protect my money for later generations and help me do good for the world today. The job appealed to Ann's zeal for solving financial puzzles and to her desire to leave the world a better place than she found it. Her previous jobs had either been in the nonprofit sector or solely focused on financial services, so she felt fortunate that she had a job that let her blend two things she loved. The perfect balance.

Ann divided her time evenly between her clients and new prospects. Her boss applauded this even split in time, but Ann's colleague Darren didn't have the same approach. Darren spent only the minimum time on his existing relationships, swooping in to address an issue when needed. Instead of Ann's steady approach to taking care of clients, Darren seemed to love the thrill of the chase. In Ann's view, he all but ignored his old customers, focusing instead on trying to bring in new, prospective clients.

Darren and Ann arrived at a three-day conference in Charleston, South Carolina, sponsored by their bank. Wealthy men and women came to the event to learn more about how they could use their assets to help their chosen charities. The event was packed with the bank's biggest current customers and several dozen new prospects who were considering making an investment there. While Ann split her time evenly between the new and the old, she noted that Darren gave superficial handshakes to his current clients and gave his deepest insights, best stories, and most reverential listening to the new prospects. Not Ann. Everybody she ran into — new prospects and existing clients — got the same, consistent level of attention.

During the weeks leading up to the event, Darren had filled his schedule for the three days in South Carolina with a marathon of one-on-one meetings with prospects — every breakfast, lunch, before-dinner-drinks, dinner, and after-dinner-drinks slot was filled. Ann spent her evenings in a group dinner with her clients and even made time to exercise each day at the hotel's gym. It was all a part of her long-term, healthy, balanced lifestyle.

After the event, Darren caught up with his current clients, his family, and his gym membership. But for those three days, he was 100 percent focused on new accounts. Darren brought in more than $50 million of new assets to the bank during the event. Ann didn't close any new deals at the event, but she deepened her relationships with her best clients. And she laid the groundwork for some new client wins over the next weeks and months.

When her boss promoted Darren to senior vice president soon after the event, Ann demanded an explanation from her boss. She told him that she was confused by the disconnect between her vaunted value of balance and the results she was seeing.

Ann had discovered the big lie of balance, which is that although executives and authors and coaches love to proclaim the benefits of balance, as Darren put it, "Executives pay lip service to balance. But they pay bonuses to people who get results." If she had been alert to it, she might also have noticed a truth about balance: sometimes what looks like imbalance (Darren's near-total focus on prospects during the three-day event) is actually part of a larger pattern of balanced priorities.

When "balance" reflects an attempt to avoid trade-offs or hard decisions by saying yes to compromise, it backfires. Leaders can say yes to two mutually exclusive choices, but *not at the same time*. You can wear the blue shirt and the red shirt, but not on the same day. What's obvious with shirts becomes more complex with everyday decisions at work. Even smart, mature leaders fall into the trap of saying "all of the above" to every multiple choice question at work.

Think about all the dilemmas you face at work. As work gets more complex and faster paced, the dilemmas pile up. Short-term versus long-term. Work versus home. Global versus local. Details versus big picture. People-oriented versus task-driven. In the face of all of these dilemmas, it's very natural to seek out a compromise. The benefits of compromise are clear: it seems more mature than picking a side. It seems to hold the promise of "something for everyone." It seems like it will, at the very least, cover your ass—with enough compromise, theoretically, you're safe against anyone who ever wants to question your judgment. Darren's move was risky; his boss might have questioned why he had ignored the current customers.

But while Ann's ass was covered in the short term, she left herself exposed in the long term. Nothing protects your career more than getting good results. If you need evidence of that, look at all the companies who shout that "how" you get things done matters too, not just what you get done. Nobody shouts that results matter, because they don't have to. Nobody shouts that results matter, because it's the most obvious thing in the world. And the problem with compromise is that it tends to lead to mediocre results. If you want winning results, you'll need to pick a bolder path.

Avoid the Allure of Unhealthy Balance

Some leaders make tough choices and achieve true distinction. For twenty-five years, Bill Gates built a software company. Then, having amassed one of the world's great fortunes through a maniacal focus on one goal—building the world's biggest and best software company—he and his wife started a new organization that is just as clear about its goal as Microsoft was. The Gates Foundation exists to "help all people lead healthy, productive lives." Bill Gates first chose to be an innovative software mogul. And then he chose to be an innovative philanthropist. He concentrated his world-class intellect and business instincts entirely on Microsoft for so long that today he has the resources to make a meaningful dent in challenges like malaria.

Instead of exhibiting the patience and discipline to do one thing at a time, many other smart leaders overreach by doing too many things at once. Even the best leaders fall into the trap of trying to be all things to all people. Here's the tragedy: they make these mistakes because they try too hard, not because they don't try hard enough. There's a voice inside the head of hard-working leaders. As the leader runs a morning brainstorm to generate new ideas with the design team, the voice ruminates on the need to drive down costs. And as the leader reads a bedtime story at night, the voice reminds the leader about the next morning's staff meeting.

The voice inside the leader's head is the internalization of powerful external cues to be balanced. In 1992, Robert Kaplan and David Norton wrote "The Balanced Scorecard," a widely influential article in *The Harvard Business Review*. The power of Kaplan and Norton's approach is the way they translate many sources of data about a business into a set of decisions that managers need to make. The Balanced Scorecard approach helps managers turn noise into signal and information into action. It has been tremendously influential, and has bolstered the idea that balance is a workplace virtue. But the generalized application of their ideas has unintended consequences for leaders. When balance is a virtue that is applied to every workplace process and leadership approach, and is left unquestioned, it can turn leaders into generalists at moments when they should be focused specialists.

The reasons why balance is misapplied and becomes unhealthy and pointless extend beyond the influence of The Balanced Scorecard movement. Some of us are what Barry Schwartz, the author of *The Paradox of Choice*, calls *maximizers*. We strive to make the right decision on everything and never settle. Schwartz and his colleagues designed choice experiments that show maximizers work to check out every option diligently, so that as the number of options goes up, so does the pain of making a choice. And as Schwartz wrote about maximizers in a *Scientific American* article, "Worse, after making a selection, they are nagged by the alternatives they have not had time to investigate. In the end, they are more likely to make better objective choices . . . but get less satisfaction from them."[1] If you're having dinner with a maximizer, be careful about giving him the wine list. On the one hand he's likely to make a very careful, considered choice. But on the other hand, he's also likely to spend the dinner lamenting over the many other options he didn't pick. Although he only gets to pick one bottle of wine at dinner, at work the maximizer solves a multiple-choice question by selecting "all of the above." As a result, he becomes unfocused. But he can always chalk up his lack of focus to balance.

Imagine you're serving tea to a room full of people. You can either serve hot tea or ice-cold tea. Half of the people in the room want their tea hot—say, 120 degrees. The other half wants their tea cold, say 40 degrees. So you do a bit of math, split the difference and serve everyone in the group tea at the average temperature: 80 degrees. Trying to find a compromise that pleases everyone usually ends up pleasing no one.

Leaders too often fall into the trap of serving lukewarm tea. This lukewarm leadership strives every day to choose everything and please everyone. Balance—the pursuit of multiple areas of focus instead of just one—has become a sacred cow. Balance is treated by leaders as if it's a good thing always. Leaders work to find balance themselves and advocate it in others.

But I believe the act of seeking balance is too often an act of cowardice—the inability to make and commit to a choice. I divide balance into two types: bland and bold. Bland balance—saying yes to everything because a leader is afraid to make a choice—leads to compromise and confusion. And most important, it leads to poor results. Bold balance, on the other hand, means making a series of tough choices that, taken together, characterize a healthy, courageously balanced leader. Balance can be a virtue, so long as it involves a series of bold choices, not the blandness of 80-degree tea.

The tug of balance comes not just from an aversion to choice, but from an attraction to bounty. Alexander Chernev, a Northwestern professor, conducted an experiment that revealed how easily we can trick ourselves into thinking more is better than less, even when it's clearly not. Picture two trays of food. The first has a full bowl of chili coated with cheese, and the second has that same bowl of chili but also a small green side salad. In Chernev's study, people who were shown only the chili guessed that it contained 699 calories, but the people who saw both the chili and the salad guessed the combined meal to contain 656 calories. And what's worse, people who identified themselves as dieters thought the salad had even bigger powers of deduction. Chernev describes his finding as "The Dieter's Paradox." On the simple objective measure of calorie estimation, the dieters consistently guessed that more food equaled less calories, so long as the extra food added balance. And so obesity rates go up, even as the number of ads touting low-calorie foods explodes. It's as if dieters think adding a few more healthy foods will reduce their total consumption.[2]

We make similar miscalculations at work, piling tasks onto our to-do list. When we work on an extra task, we might imagine we're being more productive. After all, it's more impressive to see a juggler successfully juggle four flaming torches than two. But too often our heroic attempts simply slow our progress. Research on the work output of Italian judges showed that those who work on many cases at the same time get less done than those who work on one case at a time. In their paper called "Don't Spread Yourself Too Thin: The Impact of Task Juggling on Workers' Speed of Completion," Coviello, Ichino, and Persico show that "judges who keep fewer trials active and wait to close the open ones before starting new ones dispose more rapidly of a larger number of cases per unit of time."[3] Like the judges, leaders are too often bogged down by a heavy caseload. In the name of balance or efficiency we load up our plates with too many commitments and risk overreaching to the point of dilution and inefficiency.

The Power of Bold Balance

I believe Bill Gates has led a balanced life. He continues to make important strides against poor health in developing nations and poor education in developed ones. And he built a powerful company that continues to thrive. But Gates' balance isn't the bland, 80-degree tea variety. Gates served ice-cold tea as a corporate CEO and now serves piping hot tea as a philanthropist. He makes choices. Viewed in isolation, those choices may look like decisions to be unbalanced. But over time they form a very different kind of balance. Not the bland balance of compromise, but the bold balance of brave choices.

As a leader, you can choose bland balance, bold balance, or no balance at all. The blandly balanced leader convinces himself that it's OK to chaperone his daughter to the fair, as long as he brings his smartphone with him and watches it constantly. And when he's on the Ferris wheel with his daughter, he gets an e-mail request from his boss and immediately sends a hastily written reply. *Good thing I brought my phone*, he thinks. The boldly balanced leader loses himself completely in the giddy excitement of his daughter's joy on the Ferris wheel, and the next morning he writes a clear, on-point response to his boss's note. And the leader without balance never takes her daughter to the fair.

In an article she prepared for the Harvard Business School centennial in 2008, Professor Jennifer Chatman, chair of the management department at U.C. Berkeley's Haas Business School, provides some rigor behind the notion of the bold balance. After reviewing decades of empirical research on what works for leaders, she concluded that "obvious traits such as confidence, assertiveness, or intelligence have not, as it turns out, shown the level of predictive validity that one would hope for." Instead, she revealed the three traits that could be shown conclusively to be correlated with a leader's ability to accomplish great things. The three traits Chatman cites are a strong diagnostic capacity, a flexible behavioral repertoire, and an understanding of the leadership paradox.[4]

Great leaders are great diagnosticians. Like Dr. House on the television medical drama, the best leaders have a sharp eye to see the clues to what's going on and understand the patterns those clues form, drawing on a rich database in their heads of knowledge and past experiences and the mental capability to decide what the pattern represents. Great diagnosticians can understand when a performance issue is driven by poor talent or poor management. They can tell the difference between a dangerous threat to be avoided, an interesting avenue to explore, and a once-in-a-lifetime opportunity to bet their careers on. In their book *Great by Choice*, Jim Collins and Morten Hansen get at this same phenomenon when they describe "return on luck" as the ability to recognize and take advantage of a lucky break.[5] The book shares research to show that the difference between successful entrepreneurs and those that didn't make it isn't luck—it's the ability to diagnose an opportunity as a rare bit of luck and act on it decisively.

The entrepreneurs Collins and Hansen studied did more than diagnose the opportunity. They acted on it, which gets to Chatman's second proven trait of great leaders: a flexible set of behaviors that leaders can employ as and when needed. Sometimes the leader needs to fire up the team with an inspirational speech. Sometimes the leader needs to quietly analyze a set of data and develop a point of view. And sometimes a leader needs to simply listen and validate the concerns of a team member. Just as a world-class athlete must have strength in multiple muscle groups, a world-class leader needs strength in many areas of leadership.

This is bold balance: the muscles of strength in many different components of leadership and the mind to know when to use which element. Boldly balanced leaders might look like extreme specialists in any one moment, as they show their strength in what is needed at the time. But over the long haul, they reveal a broad, balanced set of skills and traits.

I saw Chatman embrace bold balance as a teacher in a corporate setting. Every educator who teaches in a corporate environment faces the same problem: distracted students. It makes sense. In a university environment, students are paying to learn, so they have a vested interest in paying attention. Even in an MBA classroom, when students are paying to be there and can be punished by poor grades if they don't pay attention, students can still be distracted. But the corporate educator doesn't have the same incentives. I've seen some of the world's best business school professors employ dozens of techniques to fight the inevitable pull of e-mails and meetings that tugs the leader's attention out of the corporate classroom. Some of these techniques work better than others, but Jennifer Chatman is better at this than anyone I've seen.

When she started teaching a group of young managers who had been labeled as high potential, she faced a room full of distracted men and women tapping away at their laptops. With a tone full of empathy and respect, and without a hint of sarcasm, she politely suggested that many of the young leaders might have other obligations that would pull their attention away. She said it was only fair for her to let them know that the program she was about to teach was going to require their full attention, so folks who were busy should take the chance to leave now. Then she waited. When no one got up, she encouraged them again. "Surely someone must have a busy day planned," she said. And then they started leaving. Two people at first, and then a few more. She waited politely as about a quarter of the high-potential managers left the room. Those who remained were highly engaged throughout Chatman's daylong seminar on leadership. And Chatman herself never again mentioned the notion of paying attention to the workshop. Instead, she was able to stay completely present and connected to the leaders in the room.

Chatman practiced what she preached: she diagnosed what needed to be done, and she had a broad enough set of behavioral skills to act in the moment. Instead of anger or sarcasm, which some other educators would surely have shown, Chatman displayed genuine empathy. She got that it wasn't about her. Sometimes work happens, and you just can't focus on a training program no matter how interesting or important it might be. She had the courage, judgment, and confidence to act in that moment and support anyone who needed to leave. And here's a bonus: instead of making a snarky comment about the people who left the room, she pointed out to those who remained that everyone who left and everyone who stayed had themselves done exactly what she advocated: they sized up a situation and made a leadership decision to act.

I've worked with educators who exhibit the lukewarm leadership approach to that moment. They start off by pleading or insisting that no one look at their smartphones. Then several times during the day they make sarcastic remarks about any offenders. As a result, the issue of attention steals focus away from everyone in the room, and the educators seem more like nags than leaders.

Seven Steps to Make Your Balance Bold

If you strive for balance at work, you may fall into the trap of blandness and mediocrity, working to find compromises that please everyone. As a result, others at work may not view you as a strong leader who stands with courage and speaks with candor. Instead, eliminate needless compromises, build a broad behavioral repertoire, and savor the paradoxes inherent in leadership.

1. Audit for Unnecessary Compromise

The first step to striking a bold balance is to become aware of all the ways you are currently bland. Think of the dilemmas you face at work. Many leaders I work with report feeling torn between spending time reinventing new approaches to their work while also keeping their nose to the grindstone doing their current role. What are you torn between? Some describe a tool or document they use that aims to do two different things but does neither well. What are you responsible for producing that could be more distinctive and less of a compromise?

Consider the field marketing plan that a marketing manager creates to help align the field sales people around a single strategy every year. With a bit of reflection, the marketing manager realizes she uses that document for another purpose as well: to help her boss see what she does. She realizes that she's been trying to get this same poor document to do two very different things. So she decides it'll be easier and more effective if she creates two documents instead of one. The document for the sales staff will be straight to the point without wasting space summarizing research methods or explaining strategic rationale. But her boss, the chief marketing officer, needs to know that the marketing manager's plan has been thoughtful, well researched, and strategic. Now that she understands the two jobs with clarity, she creates two very different field marketing plans. One is the "tell the sales staff what to do" plan and the other is the "show my boss how thoughtful I am" plan. By uncovering and eliminating an unconscious compromise, the marketing manager improved her results and worked much more efficiently. She thought creating two documents would be more work than one, but it wasn't. Creating two documents, each with a single audience and single purpose, was a simpler task than trying to cram two different goals into the same plan. If you're trying to please two different audiences with one deliverable, consider creating two instead. It may seem like more work at first, but you'll save yourself time in the long run. Do you have a bland plan or report that would benefit from being split into two bold ones?

Or maybe it's more personal. I've met leaders who have a hard and fast work-life balance rule. For example, one man tells me he's home at 5:30 every day. It's a commitment he made to himself and his family. So he rushes home from work every day at exactly 5:30 because he promised himself he would. But most days he gets home and spends three hours half-checking e-mail and half-talking to his kids and wife. And occasionally, on slow summer days, he finds himself hanging out at the office when he could have left at 2:00 to pick up his kids from camp. Instead, he should be more boldly balanced: be a fully present dad when at home, and be a fully present leader at work.

Balance shouldn't equal compromise. If you have a team of people, sharpen up the distinction between each person's role so that they're not each doing some compromised, 80-degree-tea version of the job the entire team needs to get done. We've known the value of specialization for thousands of years, since the birth of agriculture, yet at the workplace people can naturally drift into becoming generalists.

And you don't need a team of people to replace compromise with a set of purposeful choices. Do you try to cram lots of different missions into a call just because all the right people are on the phone? In the name of efficiency, maybe you end up with mediocrity. Instead of the compromised call, have a single purpose and resist the urge to end with an open invitation to discuss anything on anyone's mind. In *The Progress Principle*, Teresa Amabile and Steven Kramer show that the most motivating thing at work is just a little bit of progress.[6] Have a short call with a single agenda item, make a decision and move on, and notice how much more motivated you feel than you do when you aim for compromise and let everyone add something to the agenda. And the other people on your call will likely value progress even over being asked if they have anything on their minds they'd like to discuss.

2. Sprint in Intervals

My athletic career in high school was limited to a couple of weeks on the cross country team. After those two weeks, my band director forced me to choose between the marching band and running, and I chose the saxophone. The eight-mile training runs weren't so bad, but I still have nightmares about the wind sprints during my short stint as a runner. Our angry, sadistic coach made us run as fast as we possibly could up a hill, then walk back down as our skinny chests heaved in search of breath. As soon as we got to the bottom, the coach screamed for us to repeat this painful cycle again. And again. Those excruciating runs made me appreciate just how much I loved playing in the marching band.

Although my coach may have been a sadist, he had science on his side. Interval training delivers more bang for the buck, from a training perspective. A high-intensity burst that takes the athlete's heart up to the edge of explosion for a few moments makes all the difference. Even the Mayo Clinic says that this approach to training is superior.[7] Just to be clear, the Mayo Clinic doesn't use the phrase "edge of explosion." And they advocate that a doctor be involved before beginning interval training. I agree. I think if a doctor would have been involved in my cross country practice our coach would have been institutionalized.

But you didn't buy this book to learn about exercise. There's an important leadership angle to the notion of interval training. Can you run a few leadership wind sprints a week? Maybe you run a wind sprint of reflection—spend a few moments of quiet contemplation simply thinking about what needs to be done. And then next run a wind sprint of innovation in which you challenge yourself and your team to develop new ideas to challenge everything. Later, run the wind sprint of realism, weeding out the unhelpful ideas.

While giving a presentation at work, ignore your kids. After all, they need you to do well at work. And give yourself permission to ignore work completely while you read a story to your kid. Put some energy into your acting performance as you read that story and you might improve your ability to put dramatic effects into your speeches at work. And even if you don't, you'll make your kid smile.

Here's the critical point—you need to train yourself to run in intervals because bold balance doesn't happen by itself. Left out on the counter, both iced tea and hot tea become room temperature. Left to the pressures of the day and the desire to be liked, leadership becomes lukewarm. Get a coach to yell at you if you need to, or else remind yourself with checklists and moments of reflection. But resist the call of compromise.

Back to Professor Chatman for a moment. When she describes the power of a flexible behavioral repertoire, she adds a cautionary note. Leaders must ground each of their behaviors and traits by demonstrating a clear commitment to the greater good, which often means the values of the organization and the best interests of others. As you perform a sequence of markedly different tasks, make sure that you—and those you lead—understand the single, coalescing purpose that connects everything you do. Without this grounding, Chatman says the leader can end up being perceived as "inconsistent, unreliable or even erratic."[8]

Bold balance doesn't equal compartmentalization. The sort of bold balance I advocate involves separate focus on one area at a time. But importantly, each area must be connected to something bigger—a larger purpose. If that's not in place, you simply have a set of disassociated traits. Compartmentalization is a form of disassociation related to behavior not in keeping with an integrated value system. Compartmentalization doesn't represent balance—it's an unhealthy pathology. To be clear, each of the leader's activities must be in concert with their value system and sense of identity. So a strict focus on operational excellence one day followed by a day spent entirely on innovation may be a great example of a leader living a bold, balanced life, so long as both operations and innovation drive toward a well-understood purpose. But one day celebrating the importance of integrity while the next day bribing a customs official to get a shipment through to an emerging market isn't boldly balanced—it's boldly lying and boldly cheating.

3. Throw Out Your Leftovers

Chris Cappy is a plain-speaking doer whose track record of results is impressive. He was a key part of the change program that helped Jack Welch when he took over GE in the 1980s and, based on Welch's recommendation, a key part of the program that helped Lou Gerstner turn around IBM in the 1990s. Cappy runs Pilot Consulting, a group that helps some of the biggest companies work their way through tricky, complex change programs with a rabid focus on results. At the heart of Cappy's approach to change is a leader's ability to act decisively.

He urges leaders to make tough choices as they drive change, which is a key element of bold balance. If you were in a leadership development program run by Cappy, he'd ask you to imagine opening your refrigerator door, hungry. You look through and find a container with leftovers from a couple days ago, shrug, and think, "it's not good enough to eat . . . but it's not old enough to throw out . . . I'll just leave it there." So the leftovers stay in the fridge for another day.

The indecision to act is what Cappy calls "food in the fridge" leadership. Leaders should reflect on a decision and then make it. There's a dozen reasons to delay a decision, and if you *want* to find a reason to hold off, you will. But delaying decisions is a cop-out strategy. Leaders are better served to follow the carpenter's maxim to "measure twice and cut once."

Is there a decision you've been delaying? Can you make a bold decision today to throw out some food that's been stuck in a corner of your
fridge for far too long? Maybe the food in your fridge is an old piece
of your identity you've been carrying around past its expiration date.
Maybe you used to be known as a data whiz or a creative genius, but it's
time to let those attachments go so you can grow more fully into your
brand as a leader. I work with many leaders at tech companies who made
their reputation as engineers. It can be a sad, difficult choice to shed that
image and replace it with a fresher leadership brand.

Picture David Carradine quoting ancient Asian wisdom in *Kill Bill*
and you get a sense of the effect Cappy has when he delivers his anec-
dotes and aphorisms. Another illustration that he uses to urge leaders to
be distinctive (this one borrowed from an old Buddhist story): "If you
are going to sit, sit comfortably. If you are going to stand, stand tall. But
whatever you do, don't wobble." I agree. Don't wobble between an old
version of yourself and a new one. Decide on an approach, throw away
your leftover plans, and then commit decisively to your new path.

4. Hold Strong Opinions Weakly

Act decisively, but stay open to new data. As you commit to a path, know
that you may need to change it. No one has better articulated how to
solve this dilemma than Paul Saffo.

Saffo, a futurist and Stanford professor, consults with companies
to help them make sense of the future. Though he doesn't pretend to
predict the future, Paul does provide many helpful ways of thinking
about it. One of his most important principles for talking about the
future — "strong opinions, weakly held" — turns out to be especially
useful for leaders in search of bold balance.

Saffo encourages forecasters to adopt a point of view with strength,
even if they have little certainty. It's much more effective to scout out all
possible scenarios if people stake out sharp, clear arguments. But here's
the key: you must be flexible enough to concede when your argument's
been disproved — that's the "weakly held" part of the principle. As he
says "The way to do this is to form a forecast as quickly as possible and

then set out to discredit it with new data."[9] Leaders need the courage to advocate a position with strength and the humility to listen to others. By doing this quickly and comfortably, conversations are more likely to lead to interesting, new, useful directions.

Here's a bland balance version of a conversation between Tom and his boss Jamie. All you need to know for context is that Tom and Jamie's company manufactures products that are sold through four distributors, and Triangle is the biggest of the four.

Tom: Triangle says if we don't give them an additional six percent margin they'll stop carrying our line.

Jamie: Triangle's important to us. We're on the razor's edge of making our numbers as it is. But I hate to be blackmailed.

Tom: I know, this is the third year they've made the same ask.

Jamie: I don't want to encourage them. But we need to make those numbers. Maybe you should go back to Triangle and see if you can get them to accept a three percent increase.

Tom: OK, sounds good.

Perfectly reasonable. Jamie has a balanced argument, and she considers and conveys both sides. Conversations like this happen every day. Neither Tom nor Jamie says anything offensive or wrong, but they also don't fully flesh out the issue. Let's see what the conversation looks like with a strong opinion weakly held.

Tom: Triangle says if we don't give them an additional six percent margin they'll stop carrying our line.

Jamie: We can't risk losing Triangle, so we need to give them the margin they ask for. It will cut into our profits, so we'll have to make up the loss in additional volume. It will force us to double down on sales efforts, and that's not a bad thing.

Tom: They're blackmailing us. We can't give them what they're asking for. It's the third year in a row. We have to stop it now or they'll never stop asking.

Jamie: Let's play this out — what happens if we walk away from Triangle?

Tom: The three other smaller distributors have been bending over back-
wards to get more of our business, so I know I can get net new
volume there.

Jamie: You can't grow those accounts by enough to make up for Triangle
in one year. They don't have the coverage.

Tom: There's a couple of new distributors who want to work with us.
We have a decent shot of making up the loss from Triangle this year.
And we'll definitely be in a stronger position next year, with wider
distribution and a tougher reputation as a negotiation partner.

Jamie: After walking away from Triangle the other guys aren't going to
push us around on margin. Maybe we can even go up a point or two
next year.

Tom: Not to mention Triangle may relent once we give them our notice
letter. But this can't be a bluff.

Jamie: Go for it. No bluff. Let's see what they do.

This time two contrasting positions smash up against each other
right at the start. Jamie takes one side strongly, and by doing so, she
encourages Tom to take the other side with strength. Truly balanced
arguments are more likely to happen when each person doesn't worry
about balance. Tom's opinion remained steadfast while Jamie's shifted.
But note that Jamie started out the second scenario with a stronger position. The strength of Jamie's position forced Tom to develop a tougher
argument, sharing more of the data, and this helped Jamie develop a more
informed point of view. This only works if Jamie has the humility and
brains to recognize a better way when it's presented to her. And it only
works if Jamie has made a genuine effort to create a trusting relationship
with Tom, so he knows that it's OK for him to truly speak his mind.

Contrasting opinions don't just lead to better decisions, they lead to
better ideas. Charlan Nemeth, working at U.C. Berkeley, tested the old
notion that brainstorms should be freewheeling exchanges in which no
idea is labeled as a bad idea. She asked groups to come up with an idea for
solving traffic problems in San Francisco. Some of the groups were told

to simply offer potential solutions without ever criticizing anyone else's ideas. Meanwhile she told other groups that they should openly critique any suggestion they disagreed with. Over and over, the test produced the same results: more critiquing produced more ideas. Perhaps we want to believe that being respectful and open creates a safer atmosphere leading to the highest creative output. But critiques seem to be more productive than support. As Nemeth and her coauthor summarized in the *European Journal of Social Psychology*: "the 'rule' of brainstorming that individuals should not criticize other group members' ideas was designed as a mechanism for increasing comfort (or lowering evaluation apprehension). Yet, this appears not to be an important element of increasing idea generation. In fact, we have previously demonstrated that such cautions may inhibit idea generation relative to an encouragement of debate, including criticism."[10]

The principle of holding strong opinions weakly can be applied more broadly, beyond conversations and brainstorms. Have a strong opinion about a career decision. Act on it decisively and follow through fully. But stay open to the signals that you need to reevaluate your path. Develop a healthy rhythm of alternating between deciding and doing, instead of staying stuck in a netherworld of in-between.

5. Build a Portfolio of Options

In addition to her role as one of the country's most successful personalities, Oprah Winfrey maintains deep, personal connections to friends she has had since she grew up in one of the toughest neighborhoods in Baltimore. Winfrey is a media executive who has achieved spectacular, consistent success without changing the fundamental nature of who she is. In the studio, she's a softie who will weep openly and make herself completely vulnerable in front of millions of people. In the boardroom she's a tough, smart negotiator who will never be taken advantage of or overpowered.

Engaged in any one pursuit, Winfrey is incredibly focused. And she manages those different pursuits so that high performance in one area does not hinder the performance of any other attribute. It is as if she has a built-in portfolio manager living in her brain. But instead of managing a balanced portfolio of stocks and bonds, the internal portfolio manager balances a portfolio of extremely focused pursuits.

Consider the metaphor a bit further. A portfolio manager hopes to have a balanced portfolio of financial assets. Some, such as treasury bonds, provide a stable return of cash flows, but little upside potential. Stock in smaller, aggressive growth companies with a relatively small market capitalization may offer the potential of upside growth, but that upside comes with considerable risk of losing value. A portfolio manager does not try to offset the risk of small cap stocks by purchasing the small cap companies who seem to present the least risk of failure—the portfolio manager typically wants the highest chance of high upside success, even if that means more risk. The manager provides balance through other assets and other classes of assets, such as Treasury bonds, which work to offset the risk of the small cap stock.

In short, portfolio managers seek the best high-risk/high-reward investments and the best low-risk/low-reward investment they can find. The result is a balanced portfolio. It would not be portfolio management at all to try to get every single asset in the portfolio to try to do the job of the entire portfolio. As long as each asset is focused on doing its particular job well, the portfolio has the best chance of achieving its overall goals.

In terms of our metaphor, some leaders need to make the transition from being a single financial asset, such as a high-growth stock, into being a portfolio manager. These leaders have been making unnecessary tradeoffs instead of bold balance. Other leaders attempt to balance their portfolio without holding any high-risk/high-reward assets—they're providing savings bond leadership in a world that needs a healthy, balanced portfolio.

6. Start a Stop Doing List

If you've ever watched the television coverage of the ball drop in Times Square on New Year's Eve, you've also seen another annual tradition: advertisements for weight loss programs. Jenny Craig and Weight

Watchers buy as much media as they can on New Year's Eve in an attempt to be the program of choice for all of the people who will resolve to lose weight starting the next morning. Gyms, diet products, and exercise equipment increase their ad buys as well. Every year, January is the best month for the hope industry.

Instead of resolving what to achieve during the year, Jim Collins urges leaders to take that opportunity to build a "stop doing" list.[11] He pointed out that his own high energy level enabled him to stay busy doing things that didn't help him achieve the long-term goals he cared about. He had to stop thinking about what he could do, and start thinking about what he should do. Jim's a rock climber who channels his boundless energy scaling up the side of steep inclines around the world. These ascents filled him with a sustaining pride that attending product review meetings didn't. So he put the meetings on his stop doing list.

Don't wait for January 1. Any day is a good day to make a stop doing list. Is there a regular meeting you can excuse yourself from? A committee you can drop out of? Are there any things you do out of a sense of fear or guilt? If so, consider taking the bold risk to stop doing them today.

7. Embrace the Paradox

We've already seen how a strong diagnostic capacity and a flexible behavioral repertoire, the first two traits Professor Jennifer Chatman advocated, can help leaders. But the third element—understanding the leadership paradox—is the most directly related to the bold balance of a leader. The paradox Chatman describes is the notion that leaders matter most when they aren't around. You've done your job as a leader when your team and organization can run without you.

Sophisticated leaders live with paradox every day. They avoid the milquetoast mediocrity of a bland compromise, embracing both bold ends of a paradox simultaneously. They don't compromise art and science, they encourage their people to do both. They don't find the third alternative between small details and big ideas: they do both.

Embrace the imbalance. Adopt the extreme ends of the new "softer" stuff you are working on. Bring your intellect to bear on your emotional challenges and ground your emotional issues in your intellect.

Perhaps no business school better represents the future of management education than the University of Toronto's Rotman School of Management. Dean Roger Martin and his team have built an entire curriculum around integrative thinking, the ability to hold two conflicting ideas in constructive tension in order to achieve an intellectual advantage. The central guiding idea behind much of Martin's curriculum design is the "dialogical mind" that can simultaneously hold opposite plans, models, and courses of action while retaining the ability to act.[12]

As kids, we like the clarity and simplicity of juice or sodas. As our palates mature, the more challenging tastes of dark coffee, earthy Bordeaux wine, or a smoky Scotch whiskey reward us with layers of flavor that unfold slowly, with complexity. So too with ideas. Performing well on a quiz on world capitals may please the young brain. But nothing provides the mature mind with such lasting pleasure as the seemingly irreconcilable paradox. Transform compromise into dialogical thinking and enjoy your intellect's ultimate treat.

Conclusion

Picture an impossibly outstretched yoga pose, a perfectly symmetrical redwood tree, and the infinite swoops of an ice skater's figure eight. Balance can be beautiful. We long for it. And leaders have a special responsibility to create an environment of balance, to provide measure and calm amidst corporate environments of instability, change, and uncertainty.

Yet we've seen in this chapter how the vision of calm, elegant balance can so easily drift into the middling mediocrity of a cowardly compromise. Stand strong, with your eyes open, and you can stand up to this quiet tug toward bland. For the courageous leader, balance isn't a safe, comfortable place to hide. It's a bold pose to strike and hold.

If you make sure you have the discipline to do one thing at a time with distinction, while holding strong opinions weakly and keeping a balanced portfolio of leadership traits, then you can become more comfortable living in the dialectical, even visionary state of bold balance.

Putting It into Practice
WHAT IS BOLD BALANCE?

Bold balance is the vision and wherewithal to avoid unnecessary compromises or trade-offs, and to effectively deploy seemingly opposing choices. The key to honoring balance as a value in the world of work is to get the timing right — to take the long view, operate sequentially, and accept that balance is dynamic, not static.

SO WHAT?

Living with seemingly paradoxical choices leads to a mature, sophisticated leadership style. Bland balance — finding a way to compromise in response to a dilemma — often stems from cowardice and confusion and leads to mediocrity and indecision. This approach backfires because compromise for the sake of compromise waters down the potency of leadership. Instead leaders must find a bold balance that preserves the value of each choice.

NOW WHAT?

1. *Audit for Unnecessary Compromise*. Seek out and eliminate the places where you currently compromise in order to avoid a tough decision. Replace the compromise with a single choice or with a portfolio approach.

2. *Sprint in Intervals*. Develop a leadership mindset of running a series of sprints instead of one long marathon. Bold balance requires sequential processing, not parallel. Get your mind conditioned for hypertasking, not multitasking.

3. *Throw Out Your Leftovers*. Decide what you want to be known for as a leader and commit to it. Don't be afraid to shed an old part of your reputation in order to move on to something bigger.

4. *Hold Strong Opinions Weakly*. Argue your point with strength, which will encourage others to argue the other side. Then allow your mind to be changed. Encouraging this kind of oppositional discourse at an organizational or team level fosters bold balance and avoids the bland compromise of groupthink.

5. *Start a Stop Doing List*. Every experienced leader has a legacy of saying yes to too many choices instead of courageously and purposefully

saying no. De-commit yourself so you can move from bland balance to bold.

6. ***Build a Portfolio of Options***. Leaders should think of the choices they have to make as a portfolio. Blandly balanced leaders try to find balance in each choice while boldly balanced leaders aren't afraid to be extreme in some choices as they build a balanced portfolio of behaviors that yields the best results over time.

7. ***Embrace the Paradox***. Seek out the paradoxes and dilemmas in your work and embrace the natural tension within them. Resist the urge to reduce dissonance into simple platitudes and instead use more dialectical thinking.

3

Automatic Accountable Collaboration

As Barack Obama campaigned for the presidency in 2008, he clung to his BlackBerry as a way to stay in touch and informed. After winning the presidency he managed to keep his favorite device despite questions about e-mail security. As the *New York Times* reported online in January 2009, "President Obama won the first fight of his presidency: he can keep his BlackBerry."[1] Fast-forward to his 2012 campaign for reelection and there were no media mentions of the President's beloved BlackBerry. Instead, the *Times* reported in August 2012 that "on most Air Force One flights, he catches up on news on his iPad." Charlie Spiering, who pointed out these differences in his Washington Examiner column, dubbed Obama the "iPad President."[2] The President isn't alone in his changing habits. The global market share of RIM, the Canadian maker of Blackberry, sank from more than 20 percent in 2008 to less than 5 percent in 2012. That's a stunning, rapid decline for a company that Fortune once described as the "fastest growing company in the world."

The CEO during RIM's dramatic tumble from greatness was Mike Lazardis. And Jim Balsillie. That's right, not one CEO, but two. In keeping with the cooperative Canadian spirit, RIM was going to teach the world a lesson in the value of collaboration, even at the very top. Lazardis founded RIM and has a deeply technical background. Balsillie is a Harvard-trained MBA who joined the company to lead sales efforts. Eventually the two decided that because the company needed both of their perspectives they should share the CEO office. During RIM's ascent, the two co-CEOs' backgrounds complemented each other well. Lazardis, "Mr. Inside," pushed the engineering teams to stay focused on improving features such as battery life and network performance. Balsillie, "Mr. Outside," kept relationships with the carriers strong. But as the market tightened and competition intensified, the lack of a single leader at the top of the company proved devastating. RIM's failed attempt to compete with the iPad shows perhaps the clearest example of the downsides of the two-CEOs-for-the-price-of-one approach.

While President Obama shifted from his BlackBerry to his iPad as his instant news device, he could have stayed in the RIM family and moved from the BlackBerry to the BlackBerry PlayBook. That's what Lazardis and Balsillie would have preferred. The BlackBerry PlayBook was launched in 2010 with much fanfare from RIM but little interest from the market. While competing with the iPad would have been tough for anyone, Lazardis and Balsillie didn't make it easier for themselves. As reported in a *Canadian Business* article, former employees of RIM say that Lazaridis ordered that the PlayBook be built for consumers. But Balsillie believed it should be sold to big businesses. "The marketing campaign positioned the tablet as 'professional grade' and yet the very name of the product suggests it's all about fun. It ultimately hit the market without meeting the needs of either consumers or business users."[3]

The PlayBook shows how the wrong sort of collaboration can lead to bland balance. The dark side of collaboration is an absence of clarity and accountability. "This co-CEO structure is almost a guaranteed model for failure," Dartmouth Business School Professor Sydney Finklestein told NPR's *Morning Edition*. "It hardly ever works. It makes it difficult to know who is in charge and I think that slowed down their ability to adapt to competitors."[4]

You'd Better Play Well With Others

Shawn, a playful kindergartener, loves the movie *Curious George*. He's drawn to the impish hijinks of the monkey more than the lessons the screenwriters work so hard to cram into the film. Jack Johnson sings on the soundtrack that "it's always more fun to share with everyone," but Shawn misses that point. The monkey makes him laugh, it doesn't teach him. Skip ahead a few years and Shawn works alone on his collage in his third-grade classroom, despite his teacher's encouragement to work with others. Everyone else in the class huddles to work together, but not Shawn. Eventually Shawn is labeled "antisocial" and forced to join the others. Shawn grows tall and lanky and is encouraged to join the middle school basketball team, where the coach emphasizes the value of teamwork over individual prowess. His coach demonizes Shawn's favorite NBA players because they're more interested in dazzling dunks instead of cooperative fundamentals like passing to a teammate. And high school is a long list of group projects and clubs. Page through Shawn's high school yearbook and you'll find his smiling face in nine different group photos, with no hint of the individualistic impulses he displayed in kindergarten. By the time he enters college he's been successfully programmed to cooperate.

When Shawn starts his first job, he's developed a habit to collaborate on everything, by default. He spends about six hours a week in various prescheduled team meetings. He works in an open-plan office or else he works at home. But even when he's at home he spends most of each day logged into virtual meetings, conference calls, or connecting with coworkers on instant messenger. Occasionally he takes breaks—to check his Facebook account.

Sometimes he has to produce something, so he books a small conference room and hides out and cranks it out. Or he takes a vacation day and works from home without connecting. He starts booking fake meetings on his calendar to avoid being pulled into conversations, and sets an "out of office" reply on his e-mail when he wants to get anything done.

The default work mode is so overwhelmingly collaborative that the rarest thing at work is the time and space required to get things done. As a result, leaders too often eat into family or personal time in order to actually get stuff done. Not too long ago, people might sneak around to *avoid* their job. Now they sneak around to *do* their job.

The Auto-Collaboration Mandate

It feels good to be a part of a team, and it's comforting to know that others are there to bolster our work when we need it. There is nothing inherently wrong with collaboration. Without collaboration of some kind, most large ventures would fail, and even the most basic family unit would fall apart. When nothing gets done without the help of a team or the input of others, then the culture of collaboration has crumbled in on itself, turning into codependent paralysis.

Workplaces weren't always so collaborative. People worked with closed doors, and meetings were a time to make decisions or hand out tasks. In the old command-and-control approach, the boss told the worker what to do and the worker obeyed or paid the price. Thankfully, management styles evolved into more sophisticated approaches that help workers become more intrinsically motivated and therefore happier, healthier, and more productive. But in some cases the pendulum swung too far—from never collaborating to always collaborating. Instead, we should collaborate when it's helpful, not because it's an unquestioned sacred cow.

Everyone has a "getting things done" muscle. Like any muscle, it must flex, or else it will atrophy. The unending reliance on the support of the team to get anything done lets that muscle sit, unused, unable to carry a heavy load when some individual act of excellence is needed. Just as sitting in office chairs all day makes workers soft around the middle, spending the majority of work connected with others weakens the productivity core.

With auto-collaboration on the rise, accountability is fading fast. When everyone is collectively responsible for something, too often no one is personally accountable for it. If things don't work out according to plan, it's too easy to blame the entire team instead of the individual. And forget about pointing to individual greatness at work — it's always the team that did it. Prioritizing team goals over individual goals means that when one person slacks off, someone else has to do additional work in order to prop up the low performer.

Nichole is a regional HR manager for a national retail clothing chain. She knows that the exit interviews the organization conducts with departing staff need a serious update, and that good data from these interviews could help diagnose and stem the company's retention problem. She mentions her idea to her manager during their weekly check-in. "That's a great idea, Nichole — why don't we bring it up with the team during the call on Thursday?" Nichole's heart sinks. Her manager's desire to "get everyone on board" for changes to systems means that everything has to be decided as a team.

On the call, her boss sets Nichole up as having an "innovative idea about exit interviews," and passes her the virtual mic. She describes the problem and a few ideas for solving it. Other HR managers listlessly agree about the retention problem, but no one is particularly enthusiastic about changing the content of the exit interview. One manager is annoyed because he doesn't have the same retention problem as the other regions and doesn't think he should have to change anything. Another manager asks who will create the survey and if they'll then be expected to do anything with the new data. As the conversation stalls, Nichole's director steps in and says, "OK, everyone e-mail your ideas about exit interviews to Nichole. Nichole, we'll talk about it in our check-in next week."

Fast-forward to the check-in the following week, and Nichole doesn't have any e-mails from anyone about the proposed changes, and time-sensitive HR issues take up most of the call. When it's time to talk about the survey project, Nichole asks if she can put together a few sample questions and pilot the new survey in her region. Her director says no, she should ask for volunteers from the team to work with her, and they can make it a priority on the call next week to approve the changes. Meanwhile, six more retail clerks have quit at two stores in her region, and nobody is collecting information about why they are leaving. She knows the matter is urgent, but she's afraid to go around the team and get things done. After all, at her last performance review her boss told her she needed to do a better job of working with others.

Nichole is afraid to rock the boat, her boss just wants to keep things afloat, and the culture at her company keeps preserving the same sentiment: consensus beats conflict, every time.

The Rare, Productive Joy of Working Alone

Meetings are ritualized collaboration, with more talking about the work than doing the work. A calendar full of meetings indicates a collaboration binge. U.C. Berkeley Professor Morten Hansen wrote *Collaboration: How Leaders Avoid the Traps, Create Unity and Reap Big* Results, which contains the most complete and compelling research on the subject of collaboration at work. Based on rigorous research into efforts to work together, he points to times and places when collaboration produces values and also to instances when it creates waste. One stunning example of waste that Hansen shares, based on academic research he did with his colleague Martine Haas, shows how collaboration can hurt sales efforts. Based on an examination of 182 teams trying to win a contract for a professional services firm, Hansen and Haas showed that the more time a team spent getting help from others, the *less* likely the team was to win a deal. The teams "assumed that collaborating with other ... experts ... would bring even more benefits," Hansen wrote. "It didn't. In fact, it brought only pain — time and effort involved in collaborating, which was time and effort the sales team did not spend making an even better bid."[5]

Hansen says that collaboration only makes sense when there is a payoff greater than the pain from collaboration. He calls this payoff the "collaboration premium." Communicating and keeping people on the same page is time-consuming and imperfect. Collaborate advisedly, only when the value of the diversity of perspectives is truly needed, not because a variety of perspectives is interesting or safe. And when people do need to work together, save the time and money spent on team-building events. Another researcher has shown that teams that get along don't necessarily get better results.

Cambridge Professor Mark de Rond has studied teams to unlock what leads to great results. "A focus on interpersonal harmony can actually hurt team performance," he says in his aptly named book *There Is an I in Team: What Elite Athletes and Coaches Really Know About High Performance*.[6] De Rond is a sacred cow tipper of the first order, taking on Daniel Goleman, author of *Emotional Intelligence*. Where Goleman celebrates the importance of team harmony, de Rond lauds internal competition as an important but underappreciated ingredient in team success. Too often, complains de Rond, experts point to the virtues they hope to be important, such as collaborating nicely with your team members, instead of simply reporting the facts of the case, as discomfiting as they may be. From a retail store chain in the United Kingdom to surgeons in Afghanistan to improv comedians, de Rond documents how helpful internal competition can be to long-term positive outcomes.

The biggest benefit to a culture that focuses on the "work" half of teamwork is that as collaboration goes down, accountability goes up. Rather than diffusing accountability across the group, individuals are accountable for outcomes. Groups within organizations can still be collectively accountable for results, but when goals are set for individuals it's easier to spot the weak link in the system.

The point is not to highlight the struggles of underperformers, merely to shame them. The point is to break team members out of the habits of learned helplessness and create patterns that flex the right muscles at the right time. Leaders must face their own fears and trust their own and others' ability to do the work. Stepping back and allowing others to struggle is one of the hardest tenets of leadership, but it's necessary for growth. Allowing for growth doesn't preclude training, coaching, and support — it just means that in the end, everyone must be responsible for their own piece of the puzzle.

Being alone by default also values and savors collaboration when the time is right. If everyone is working independently toward specific outcomes, the areas where collaboration is necessary become inescapably clear. Putting everyone together all the time means that the instinct to collaborate trumps the need to collaborate, and it becomes unclear who or what can really contribute to results. Collaboration has a cost, and leaders must calculate that cost each and every time they choose to collaborate. It's time to plant a new decision tree in your brain: is the outcome worth the cost of this collaboration?

Seven Steps to Make Your Collaboration Accountable

To lead more accountable collaboration, you'll need to seek out lazy collaboration by default and eliminate it. Then ruthlessly destroy the teams that exist without a clear purpose and the meetings that happen without an important point. Finally, design new approaches to collaboration on an as-needed, just-in-time basis.

1. Audit to Eliminate Automatic Collaboration

Fish school together in a "bait ball" to avoid a predator because lonely fish are easier for sharks to snag. In the same way, workers cluster around an idea to avoid the risk of standing out. As a leader, look for the signs that people are working together as a way to validate their thinking. There's safety in numbers. Do as much as you can to limit the existence of the rote check-ins that people use to make sure they're on the same page. Innovation and productivity need different people making real progress on different pages. Being on the same page is overrated. You'll know necessary collaboration when you see a team with a clear achievable purpose, a plan to disband when the mission is achieved, and you know what each person on the team has committed to deliver. In that case, enjoy the productivity that comes with accountable collaboration.

Are you on "teams" that are simply a group of people who report to the same supervisor? Sheera is.

Sheera was tasked to run the weekly team meetings while her boss was away for two weeks, and by noon on the day of the first meeting, she panicked. She called a trusted colleague on the team and asked, "I'm worried I don't have enough agenda items to fill up the whole hour." Sheera and her boss need to do a serious assessment of the purpose of the weekly team meeting. Is the aim to accomplish anything at all, or simply to be on the phone for an hour together? The team doesn't even get the benefit of seeing each other in person or on video; they just honor the sacred cow of collaboration while ignoring the ever-present need to get things done.

Even the most charitable people do what's necessary to look after their own affairs — paying the bills, putting food on the table, maintaining a safe and healthy life. Your own time and energy make up your most-precious currency at work, so it is unwise to give it all away before you take care of the necessities.

Turn the collaboration equation upside down, not just for yourself, but for anyone who has been participating in the "all hands on every deck" mentality with you.

2. Make Teams Temporary

In 1963, Marvel Comics created its first superhero collaboration, *The Avengers*. The makeup of the team changed throughout the four decades of its original run, but one thing never changed: "Earth's Mightiest Heroes" joined up to fight the foes no single superhero could fight alone. The popular franchise swept the box office in May 2012 with Joss Whedon's *The Avengers*, bringing together Iron Man, The Hulk, Captain America, Black Widow, Thor, and Hawkeye to thwart an evil plot to destroy Earth. This motley crew struggles to gel at first, but eventually their common purpose overcomes resistance and they work together to save the planet from certain doom.

The most important lesson from *The Avengers* is not to form teams of cantankerous misfits who don't really like each other. The point is: assemble reluctantly. Collaborate only when the danger from not collaborating is clear and present. The team only joins up when they must tackle a problem or an enemy so great that no single hero can get it done on their own. When they eventually save the world, they tighten up any loose ends, put their metaphorical stamp on it, and scatter back to their homes around the globe. They don't call to check in, they don't plan an annual meeting, and they mostly hope never to see each other again.

Teams at work should consider this approach. Assemble with the end in mind and pick an expiration target based on achieving the team's goal. A group of people who report to the same manager or who share a job title are not, by this definition, a team. A team must have a time-bound purpose that is their reason for existing, and that purpose shouldn't be "because we have the same boss." Too often when people who report to different managers are pulled together to achieve some-thing, organizations slap a distracting name on them: a virtual team, a task force, a tiger team—or worse, a committee. These names are distracting because they obscure the truth that these should simply be real teams formed to achieve a real solution.

Real teams have real purpose, and leaders clearly and regularly state the purpose. At checkpoints leaders should ask: What was our origi-nal purpose? Does that purpose still make sense? If not, how should we change? Why should we continue as a team? As long as the answers reflect the original purpose of the team, the assembly remains intact. If the team is no longer serving the purpose, it is time to disband.

Leaders must fight the natural inertia of teams who come together and stick together out of habit. When teams feel an easy camaraderie they may linger longer than they provide value. Treat these teams with healthy skepticism. Collaboration can make team members feel too cozy. Contributors should feel, instead, that their participation could end at any moment, and they should look forward to the end, because it means that they have done their part.

Think about the teams you lead or belong to. Is there an end in mind? Is there a point at which you can put a finishing stamp on the work and move on? Or do your teams exist for some common trait instead of a common task? Are you "checking in" with team members for the sake of checking in, rather than creating a litmus test for team partici-pation? Would leaving the team cause stigma or shame? It's the leader's job to focus on the purpose of the team, and purpose should be the only reason anyone should continue. Alone must be the default state of work, and the ultimate goal of a team should be to achieve its mission so it can break up.

3. Let Underperformers Sink or Swim

Liz and David work in business development for a consultancy based in Boston. Liz works remotely from Indiana, while her East Coast counterpart, David, sits at headquarters and has a reputation for only stepping it up when a senior leader has his or her eye on a project. This infuriates Liz, as she is not only incredibly productive from her home office, but often has to step in for David when he doesn't deliver on time, which is most of the time. David is a smooth talker and always verbally takes responsibility for his missteps, assuring Liz and others that his behavior is "unacceptable"—yet continues to behave in precisely the same way over and over again. Liz and David's supervisor, Ella, is a classic auto-collaborator, focusing on the team's collective responsibilities and not the individual contributions that make up the results.

Liz has been tasked with leading a project to create short, informative profiles of the seven lines of business in the consultancy. Given Liz's current workload, Ella knows it's impossible for Liz to do all seven herself, so she suggests Liz divide up the profiles between herself and David. She's not happy about it, but Liz relents and assigns him the three simplest ones. She does everything in her power to set David up for success: she creates a template for the profiles, she walks him through the steps of research and profile writing, and she puts two milestone dates on his calendar. David is an intelligent, experienced professional who is more than capable of completing this basic task, yet when the first milestone arrives, he hasn't even scheduled the required in-house interviews. "I'm sorry, Liz, I know this is unacceptable, but I've been swamped and just haven't been able to make time for this." Liz is steaming mad: her four profiles are complete and David hasn't even begun.

I don't need to tell you how this story ends—it was over before it began. Liz eventually takes back the three profiles, completes them, and submits the package to the VP. Ella praises Liz for her sacrifice for the team, and David lives to see another day where he's not held accountable for anything he doesn't want to do. Liz has brought up David's failure to contribute once a quarter for three years, yet David continues to grow and thrive in the organization, and Liz continues to do his work. If she ever wants anything to change, she has to face the potential discomfort of not just calling David out on his shortcomings. She must let him fail. Every time Liz intervenes, she simply reinforces the fact that he doesn't actually need to do anything that he doesn't feel like doing. Every time Ella praises Liz for saving the day, accountability takes a hit. Where there's enablement, there's laziness. It's best for everyone to call out laziness when you see it. Don't let it linger — not in others and certainly not in yourself.

I am in no way suggesting you do not set your team up for success, but it is a leader's duty to hold individuals accountable, no matter what. Allowing someone to feel the pain of letting you or the team down is healthy. Either the slacker learns that he must finally step up — or a public display of his shortcomings forces change.

4. Stay Aligned with the Bigger Picture

Once you understand the nature of your team and focus on the accountability of its members, it's time to take a step back and assess the purpose of the team in the larger context of the organization. Leaders must not only be accountable and hold others accountable, but must hold team purpose accountable to company mission and direction. The last thing a successful leader wants is to be on a zombie team, aimlessly wandering around and snacking on the brains of more important resources.

The newly instated CEO of your multinational software company tasks you and a small team with increasing the autonomy of each country leader in the organization. Your team focuses for three months on enabling and empowering the regional leaders, when a sudden market downturn causes the CEO to announce a cost-cutting initiative. The stubborn, non-purpose-driven team would continue on its mission to bolster the position of each country leader despite the change. The average team would continue to find ways to enable country leaders, but will add a cost-savings commitment to each proposal. The accountable team, however, knows that in lean times, individual autonomy must step aside in favor of efficiencies. You don't waste any time being emotional or waiting to be told of the new priorities; instead, the team disbands and you set about forming a new team that is focused on cost-cutting measures. Some team members might not make sense for the new initiative or won't want to go along, but that's fine; the goal is to align team purpose with organizational vision, not to make individual team members feel important or needed.

This is not as easy as it sounds, and leaders must be vigilant in constant assessment of team purpose. Leaders must not align their own identity or purpose with the purpose of a team; if teams are meant to be disassembled when the goal is met, they must be just as willing to disband or change direction when strategy calls for it. To successfully navigate these kinds of changes, leaders must overcommunicate from the start the natural fragility of a team's structure.

Four-Star U.S. Army General (Ret.) Stanley McChrystal took this topic quite literally. Instead of using traditional materials to build the massive quarters needed to host American military leadership in Iraq and Afghanistan, he insisted that everything be built out of plywood. "We built everything out of plywood," he told *The Daily Beast*, "and we did it because you can do it very very quickly and you can do it very inexpensively and you could rip it apart and redo it so the function of your organization was shaped by the form and you could change it as often as you needed to."[7] While leaders may not need to change the physical structure of office buildings in order to quickly change direction as a team, we can all take a page from what General McChrystal calls "plywood leadership." Never consider the structure or purpose of a team to be permanent, and know that you can and should use the same materials to create something new and more relevant at any time.

This kind of willingness to adapt will not go unnoticed in the organization. Inspire team members to think of their place on the team as temporary, and ask them to join you in your focus on aligning purpose and vision. Be willing to decouple your own identity or the identity of a team with the work; simply be known as a leader or a team that moves swiftly and agilely in whatever waters you encounter.

5. Own Your Results

"Do what you say you are going to do, when you say you are going to do it." This might seem like a gimme, but in an environment of auto-collaboration, you'd be surprised at how often the basic concept of individual accountability gets swept under the rug of the "team." If teams are created with a purpose and leaders are vigilantes for unnecessary components, however, individuals should never have any doubt what they are expected to do and when and how they are expected to deliver it. Being a leader or a member of a team should link directly to outcomes and this is when you get to flex your "getting things done" muscle.

Stuff happens. You miss the mark. Being accountable to the team means not just delivering results, but forcing yourself to face and endure the pain of not doing what you were supposed to do. What happens when you don't deliver is just as important as the other 99 percent of the time when you do. A leader can undo months or years of account-ability by just once leaning on the team to step in when she falters. Being accountable means owning all results, not just the good ones.

Super Bowl XLVI did not end well for the New England Patriots. They were up 17–15 against the New York Jets in the fourth quarter when quarterback Tom Brady threw a potentially game-sealing pass to wide receiver Wes Welker. Welker had to jump in the air and con-tort his body to receive the ball, and despite a glowing record as a receiver on this championship team, he failed. The Jets took the lead and eventually won the game, and Patriots fans were understandably furious with Welker for missing the crucial catch. Moments after the defeat, Tom Brady's wife, supermodel Gisele Bundchen, got in front of the cameras and publicly blamed Welker and the other receivers for not catching her husband's passes. Brady and Welker had a choice here, and instead of blaming each other for the miss, each player took respon-sibility for his part in the gaffe. It didn't make Patriots fans feel any better about the loss to the Jets, but this is what it means to be personally accountable to the team.

Making excuses or blaming the team for not getting something done is like the quarterback who blames the receivers. The quarterback is responsible for throwing the ball and is only held responsible for his own passes. The other team's defense will surely be in the way, and blaming an interception on anything other than one's own lack of foresight on the field falls short of what's necessary for accountable collaboration. Just as there is no football game without another team, there is no work environment without competition, distractions, or any number of circumstances that can get in the way of results.

Sometimes enablement happens when leaders recognize their own behavior in others. Reinforce the bad behavior before your own gets called out, and you're essentially enabling yourself. I recently taught a group of experienced managers at Cisco and watched this happen live. One participant boldly asserted that he participated in calls that he shouldn't because he just wanted to be in the know, and his involvement probably led to less autonomy from the managers he managed. The other participants in the room perked up and immediately defended the confession, saying that it was important that he be in the know. Here was this bold man, stepping up and being accountable for his actions, and everyone around shut him down to avoid looking in the mirror.

6. Hunker Down

As a young manager working inside Duke Corporate Education I had a team of three people reporting to me. My boss worked with me to think about how to best develop those three. The two junior team members were easy: focus on planning, execution, communication, and so forth. One of my employees was a very talented guy who had quickly shown he could get good results managing client relationships, managing projects, designing programs, and teaching. I figured the only issue with the bright young guy was how to keep him engaged and happy with work. But my boss suggested something different. My boss said he was too isolated from the rest of the company. Sure, he'd achieved a lot. But his achievements had come at the expense of visibility across the broader organization. Everyone knew he was a nice guy, but nobody knew quite how bright he was. Too often he worked in a hidden conference room in the basement of the building with his headphones on, quietly getting work done. My boss said she had been given some of the same advice by the top leaders at Duke CE.

My employee left Duke CE after writing a best-selling business book. To be fair to my boss, she was right. Leaders are wise to lift their heads up and get noticed. But what I've found is people are a lot happier to notice you if you've accomplished something distinctive. And to do that, you may need to hide out alone to get things done. In workspaces designed for openness this can seem like an act of rebellion. You might even need to take a sick day and stay home to get something done—better than swimming with the tide of chitchat at the office.

In too many organizations visibility is commonplace but achievement is rare. The accomplishment of both is rarer still. Some leaders debate the importance of relationship-focus versus task-focus. I believe that's a false choice. The accountable leader gets things done that matter, and those accomplishments help build relationships based on respect, not popularity. The best leaders know they must occasionally hunker down and concentrate intensely, ignoring any voice in their head that is urging them to be more visible.

People sometimes confuse meetings with leadership. They think that individual contributors hunker down and knock things off the list, but once you get promoted to a certain level of leadership, you run meetings and inspire others to "do the work." Everyone needs to hunker down, no matter how big your job is. Increased seniority simply means leaders must sometimes hunker down to do higher-level work. Former GE CEO Jack Welch would spend an hour each day in what he called, "looking out the window time." He knew if he didn't protect that hour for thoughtfulness, for hunkering down and focusing, he would spend his entire day in meetings. Even if it's only an hour, protecting your time in order to get things done is the best way to model accountable collaboration. It shows your people that you respect them enough to contribute more than just words at a meeting.

How you hunker down is up to you. You might need to work from home one day a week. You might need to block the first hour of your day to focus on how you plan to meet your goals. Or reconsider the arrangement of the office and how much face time you give to the organization. Continue to build relationships, but do it by demonstrating the value of your achievements. Setting aside focused work time and adhering to it protects the most valuable asset you have in an organization, which is your reputation.

7. Unplug

Even if you turn the collaboration equation upside down and focus on being "alone by default," it's still easy to trick yourself into believing you're alone when you're really not. If you are working with your smartphone next to your laptop, with your instant messenger client on and e-mail notifications popping up at regular intervals, then you may be physically alone, but you haven't unplugged. The autonomy that comes from producing without constant feedback or validation — that's the autonomy that's needed in order to do your best work.

I'm not talking about going into your cave for six months or six weeks, but it's amazing how much you can get done on a six-hour flight. I remember talking to a retired English media executive about his approach to vacation. He never took less than three weeks at a time because, he said, "It takes a week to get work off of your mind, then you've got a week to relax, and by the third week you're ramping back up for your return to the office." Not all of us are so lucky as to have six weeks of vacation time a year, but he had the right approach. It takes more than a few hours of working alone to get to the good stuff. Take the time. Scale the approach up or down to fit your schedule. Take a sick day if you need to, but find a way to escape the tug of automatic collaboration.

As a manager, you might need to let your direct reports take a day of solitude to finish a project, no matter how much you wish they would stay on e-mail when they work from home. Allowing your team to unplug demonstrates your trust in them and your respect for their autonomy.

The CEO of the company I described in Chapter One, Julian Fletcher's former boss, summed it up nicely. She said when she founded a company and it really started to grow, she stopped using headphones when she went to the gym. She said she needed to listen to herself. Running a company, supporting her family, and volunteering meant that there was little time for solitude. She might not be able to spend six days working on her own, but at least for the ninety minutes she's at the gym, she is undistracted and unplugged.

Conclusion

People rise or fall to meet the expectations you have of them. It's the mantra of the highest-performing schools across the nation—high expectations lead to high achievement. Teams must exist for a purpose, and leaders must hold themselves and their team to the highest expectations. I don't advise you to collaborate less because other people don't need you, and I don't suggest you work alone because your team just isn't that helpful. I push for rare and special collaboration because the truth is that you, alone, are capable of much, much more than you might expect.

When you're thinking of collaboration, remember *The Avengers*. They only came together for a purpose so large that it could never be handled alone, and they disassembled as soon as the task was done. Even as they were defeating the evil space invaders, they still mostly worked alone, each individual doing the work they were best suited for. Teams must have a purpose, and if the purpose changes, the teams must change. There is no greater danger to productivity than the standing committee meeting—a team for the sake of a team, a meeting for the sake of a meeting. Hold everyone accountable, including yourself, and set aside the time and space you need to get things done.

Putting It into Practice
WHAT IS ACCOUNTABLE COLLABORATION?

Accountable collaboration is working together with clear consequences for underperformance and clear commitment from each team member to the team, and a clear, time-limited purpose from each team to the organization. The key to honoring collaboration as a value in the world of work is to default to working alone, only collaborating when necessary, and fostering a culture of trust and universal accountability.

SO WHAT?
Automatic collaboration leads to underperformance and low productivity for the sake of playing well with others. Teams that exist because of structure and not purpose waste time and enable learned helplessness and group-think. Too often everyone is involved and no one is responsible.

NOW WHAT?
1. ***Audit to Eliminate Automatic Collaboration.*** Ask the right questions about teams and meetings: What is the purpose? Who really needs to be involved? Does this team still make sense?
2. ***Make Teams Temporary.*** The ultimate goal of a team should be to disband. Use regular checkpoints to assess whether or not individuals are still needed on the team. And plan for the end in advance, to give the team purpose and urgency.
3. ***Let Underperformers Sink or Swim.*** Allowing someone to fail helps them get better or helps them to get out. Stepping in for the good of the team blocks growth and reinforces bad behavior.
4. ***Stay Aligned with the Bigger Picture.*** The purpose of the team should always reflect the vision and strategy of the organization. If company purpose changes, team purpose must also change. Don't be on a zombie team that doesn't contribute to the ultimate goal.
5. ***Own Your Results.*** Do what you say you are going to do, when you say you are going to do it. Don't get caught up in the team's dysfunction, and relentlessly model what it means to meet expectations.

6. ***Hunker Down.*** Take the time to do the work and be recognized for accomplishments, not personality. Build relationships by being reliable, not just nice.

7. ***Unplug***. It is nearly impossible to turn off your access to the world and the world's access to you, but it's imperative to get to your best thoughts. Go into your cave for however long it takes and resist the temptation to get outside validation.

4

Narcissistic Useful Creativity

In 1996, I was twenty-four and excited to be working at a public relations firm in Boston. While my cubicle had a view of the bathroom door, the main conference room had a view of the Charles River from the sixteenth floor. The best part of my job was finding any excuse to work or meet in that conference room. I started working in PR because I enjoyed writing and talking and I wanted to be a part of a creative environment. Staring at the sailboats that glided between Cambridge and Boston met more of those creative needs, I suppose, than calling reporters to make sure they received the press release I just faxed them.

Though the firm's client base had been primarily consumer companies based in New England—Ocean Spray and Hasbro, for example—high-tech start-ups started to call on the firm soon after I joined. I had a little bit of computer programming experience in high school and was a young guy with glasses who could program the fax machine to remember ten fax numbers, so I logically stepped into the role of high-tech PR guru. This was going to be fun—finally, my chance to put my creative muscles to good use.

My first high-tech client was Vivo Software, a videoconferencing start-up led by Staffan Ericsson. Dr. Ericsson was a brilliant Swedish scientist who, while completing his doctorate at the Royal Institute of Technology at Stockholm, patented the first technology to convert analog video into a digital file that even the slow PCs of the mid-90s could handle. Vivo had the technology that could bring video to the web. This was just three years after the web got graphics and one year after it got its first audio streams, so web-based video was hard to imagine. In the dial-up world of 28.8 modems hardly anyone predicted today's world of videoconferencing from an iPhone. But Dr. Ericsson saw it coming. In a September 1995 article in *Network Computing* he said that "the incremental cost of adding videoconferencing will be a couple of hundred dollars. At that price, people will even start using it for fun."[1] That seemed like a crazy idea. At the time, videoconferencing was a very expensive corporate service that only the richest companies could splurge on. Who knew that eventually it would be free?

With a budget of just $30,000, Dr. Ericsson asked our firm to help reposition Vivo's technology from a business-to-business tool to a consumer platform for streaming video over the Internet. The project was small enough that a team comprising just two other young guys and myself could run things on our own without much adult supervision. The grown-ups were taking care of the big companies, so we could fly under the radar. We targeted Spring Internet World '96, a trade show happening in Silicon Valley in just a few weeks. I had never been a part of a trade show, so this was a great chance for me to finally let my creativity soar.

Our first creative idea was Vivo Man. The logo for Vivo was a purple upside down triangle with the "VIV" at the top and the "O" filling up the bottom.

The effect looked vaguely human, with the Vs as eyes, the "I" as a nose and the "O" a wide-open mouth. We had a purple spandex costume made, with a giant Disney-character-size triangle head for our Vivo Man. I contacted the theater department of a college in San Jose and requested a tall, heroic college student to fill out our costume, which was designed to fit a tall, heroic Vivo Man. When we arrived at the outdated Best Western Hotel in Sunnyvale, California, my first thought was: "So this is the technology hub of the Universe?" Things went downhill from there.

The next morning we met our Vivo Man actor outside of the San Jose Convention Center. I'm not sure how this happened, but he was much shorter and rounder than I had been led to believe. In the purple spandex costume, the effect was more comical than heroic. I had imagined a high-tech superhero, but instead found a creepy Barney. But we had no choice, so we trudged on into the center. As we did, we were immediately greeted by a serious young woman wearing a stern expression. She asked if we had paid a character appearance fee. That was a $10,000 expense I didn't know about and couldn't afford. So we turned Vivo Man around and left him across the street at a bus stop to walk around and wave at the people as they entered the show. With his bulging beer belly and extra-long purple footies dragging behind him, this was not the cutting-edge image that Dr. Ericsson had hired us to project.

Luckily, we did one thing that worked, and it was perhaps the least creative thing we did. Instead of simply having a booth to demo our product, we used the technology to report on the event as if we were a news company. The new technology could be used to post video interviews online and stream them out in real time, so why not put the technology to use? We called ourselves VVN, borrowing from CNN, and set up our "studio" at the cheapest booth space on the floor. Before the event we secured media credentials, the same badges that *The New York Times* and *NBC-TV* got. With the badges came a list of who would be attending the show. We checked with Dr. Ericsson to see whom he most wanted to speak with and arranged interviews with those people at our studio on the trade show floor. He sought investors who could provide Vivo with enough money to complete their transformation from videoconferencing company to web start-up. Several venture capital firms and executives at large technology companies agreed to be interviewed.

I appointed myself the title of senior producer of VVN and interviewed our targets about the event and the future of the Web. At the end of each interview, I asked the magic question, "Would you like to see what you look like online?" This would have marked the first time many of these people saw themselves in a streaming video on a computer, and the novelty was too much to resist. In short, we demonstrated the technology, which is the most basic, obvious thing to do at a trade show.

One of the people who watched his own interview was an executive with Progressive Networks. Progressive made an investment in Vivo after the show, and two years later they bought the entire company. Progressive Networks became Real Networks, and their product, Real Video, was the dominant online video streaming product by 2000.

The lesson for me? Our crazy idea of Vivo Man was really just about our own narcissistic urge to do something different. It didn't make business sense. And don't bail us out and suggest that the idea might have been good but the execution was poor. I'm sure now both were bad. Even if we had paid the appearance fee and made sure we had a perfectly proportioned actor, the idea would have had little impact. In fact, at lunchtime I went to check on Vivo Man and found our actor with his giant purple mask off taking a cigarette break, which was fine. Keeping Vivo Man off the show floor was the best thing that could have happened. The idea that worked was the one that simply involved combining two existing ideas: news coverage *of* an event and product demonstration *at* an event. Covering the event using the video technology seemed like the most obvious idea in the world, so it didn't feel as good to create. But Dr. Ericsson wasn't paying $30,000 to help us feel creative. As silly as our youthful mistake might look now, there are seasoned executives today still stuck in the trap of narcissistic creativity. Consider, for example, Sony.

Tokyo-based *New York Times* reporter Hiroko Tabuchi highlights Sony's place among Japan's faltering tech sector, saying in an April 2012 article that Sony must "fight for its life" despite an "astonishing lack of ideas."[2] Tabuchi charts Sony's decline from a position of leadership in consumer electronics to barely hanging on. Tabuchi isn't alone. Newspapers, magazines, and business books have also highlighted the shame of Sony's inability to generate anything standard-worthy since the Trinitron TV and the Walkman, both of which are relics of the last century. So Sony failed because of a lack of creativity. Right?

Wrong. In fact, Sony's failures stem from too much creativity. Instead of listening to the market with humility, Sony's engineers crammed their best technology into an MP3 player that was too cumbersome to use. Instead of taking care of their customer's needs for simplicity, they took care of their own engineer's need for complexity. Engineers inside Sony viewed the storage technology used by Apple's iPod as boring and beneath them, and so they went their own way. These innovators had brains full of ideas. Their problem wasn't too few ideas: their problem was too much narcissism. Proud Sony engineers joined the company to invent industries in Japan that would lead the world, not imitate innovations coming from Korea, China, or America. They wanted to invent something new as part of their legacy.

With the advent of the individual electronic music track in the late 1990s, Sony had everything it needed to create a transformational entertainment product. But rather than adapting to what the market wanted, Sony created something new. Instead of learning from the market, they tried to teach it. This is not evidence of a shortage of ideas. It's a failure of leadership.

Sony's issue is just an outsized version of what leaders face every day. When leaders are creative just for the sake of innovation, for an ego boost or a moment of self-congratulation, creativity backfires.

Scratching the Itch of New

Teresa Amabile is, among other things, a guru of creativity. Since her seminal work in the early 1980s she's helped the world think critically about how creativity works. She's on the faculty of Harvard Business School and continues to think about, study, and share her findings on creativity. Amabile defines creativity as the "production of novel and useful ideas in any domain."[3] So if it's not useful, it's not creative. But leaders too often celebrate an idea for its novelty alone, without regard to its usefulness. What passes for creativity in the workplace is often merely a new idea. Engineers don't get patents for using someone else's idea, and CEOs don't get on the cover of magazines for pragmatically adopting another leader's approach. Novelty generates more social rewards than usefulness, so leaders tend to discount the usefulness of old options and overvalue new ones.

Scott Barry Kaufman, a New York University cognitive scientist who studies creativity, says our search for the unexpected is both deep-seated and endless. "If you present an idea as new," he says, "people will get a dopamine hit, regardless of whether or not the idea is true or good. This is why it's important to use conscious thought to contemplate the automatic emotional consequences of the dopamine rush and decide whether or not the idea really is effective or whether it's just designed to scintillate."[4]

If you ignore Kaufman's advice, you may overestimate how much you'll enjoy something new. Imagine you stop and get a coffee every day on your way to work. There are two shops side by side, Mario's and Emil's. You've tried both and prefer Mario's. Imagine on January 1 you have to plan out your coffee consumption for the coming year. Once you commit, you have to stick to the plan. How many times will you allow yourself to stop by Emil's? Even though you know you prefer Mario's, losing the option to ever go to Emil's is painful. Typically people faced with the choice to do only one thing won't commit exclusively to one option, but will later regret that choice. We think we never want all of our eggs in the same basket, but sometimes we do.

This tendency to overestimate how much variety will satisfy us is called "diversification bias" and was first studied by Daniel Read and George Loewenstein while at Carnegie Mellon.[5] Read and Lowenstein's experiments show how we think we want more variety than we end up wanting. They did many studies on a wide range of subjects, but my favorite was their Halloween experiment. The candy that a trick-or-treating kid chooses is a very serious decision, and one that yields important insights into our natural human preference for novelty.

In the experiment, two neighbors conspired to systematically vary the choices kids could make. Some randomly selected kids got to pick two candy bars at one house, but none at the next-door neighbor's house. Another group of kids, meanwhile, got one candy bar at each house. At both houses the kids were picking from a bunch of Three Musketeers™ and Milky Way™ candy bars. Every one of the kids who picked two candy bars at the same time picked one of each. But less than half of the kids who got one candy bar at each house got one of each. Considered separately, the kids picked their favorite candy bar twice. But the kids who had the chance to pick two bars at the same time opted for diversity. There was no payoff to their diversity, though. They merely ended up with less of their favorite. Back at home, enjoying their Halloween bounty, kids eat their favorite candies first, of course. As the authors report about anyone who predicted they'd appreciate more variety than they usually do: "They first consume the goods they prefer the most and then turn to the less desirable items."[6]

We grown-ups look for new candy bars at work. Our natural tendency to overestimate how much we'll prefer variety has been shown in several other experiments across adults. Because of the diversification bias, we seek out something new to add to our portfolio of projects. New must be better than old, right? Think of Sony and their thousands of new products from video game players to TVs to music. Meanwhile Apple's entire product line can fit on a kitchen table. One of those, the iPhone, accounts for more revenue than Sony's entire annual sales. Both companies are creative, but Apple seems to have more of a maniacal focus on useful creativity.

Creativity should be pragmatic, not prideful. When it's pragmatic, creativity exists to solve an important, unsolved problem. When it's prideful, it exists to boost the ego of the creator. Narcissistic creativity doesn't just waste the narcissists' time. Think of the leader who puts on a dazzling magic show of idea generation. It's impressive to witness these acts of genius. The problem is, when a magician is in the room, everyone else becomes part of the audience. Creative people leave us impressed with them, eager to watch the next magic show.

Don Draper, the charismatic ad agency creative director on AMC's *Mad Men*, works his magic in a 1960s workplace. When he bids to introduce Kodak's slide projector wheel, the Carousel, he tells the prospective clients, "The most important idea in advertising is new. It creates an itch. You simply put your product in there as a kind of Calamine lotion." But Draper goes on to suggest that Kodak should position its product as nostalgic, because creating nostalgia creates a sharp pain that the product can relieve. As he goes on, Don uses the carousel to show charming pictures of his own family as they grew up, including his own wedding pictures. But we know those family pictures betray Don's constant womanizing. It's part of the genius of Matt Weiner — *Mad Men*'s creator — to use the charismatic power of creativity to force the audience to reconsider notions of virtue and vice. How can someone who behaves so badly be so likable? Part of the mix of Don's richly irreconcilable character is his irresistible creativity.

Watch out for the narcissists at work — research shows them to be clinically charming. As researchers from Stanford and Cornell showed in a 2010 study, it's easy to be tricked into thinking you've seen creativity when you've just seen charm. Students who rated highly on tests of narcissism had their pitch for a new movie idea rated more highly than their more humble counterparts. But when independent assessors rated the written version of the ideas, the narcissists' ideas were rated to be no better than the rest. As the authors of the study put it, "Although narcissists do not necessarily generate more creative ideas, they are able to convince others that [their] ideas are more creative because their high levels of confidence, enthusiasm, and charisma correspond to commonly held prototypes of the creative personality."[7] So what looks and feels like creativity may simply be narcissism.

Creativity, and its corporate cousin, innovation, propel leaders to success in business and life. Without them, nothing would change, and our lives would be an endless series of frustration and a lack of learning.

With narcissistic creativity, however, leaders can harm their business just for the short-term payoff of good feelings and congratulations.

In his book *The Upside of Irrationality*, Duke economics professor Dan Ariely describes how Thomas Edison was fueled by his own narcissistic creativity, denying that Nikola Tesla's alternating current (AC) was a better global energy solution than his own direct current (DC). Despite the opportunity to profit greatly from Tesla's work (Tesla worked under Edison when he invented AC), he couldn't admit that his protégé's idea was superior to his own. If you've ever plugged anything into a wall in your home, then you know how doomed Edison's narcissistic creativity turned out to be: AC was the scalable power solution that the world needed.[8] As Edison's eventual commercial success demonstrates, narcissistic creativity can be overcome, through persistence and, as Edison put it, perspiration. But I think that in the past hundred years or so, we've learned a few things that can help narcissists recover without so much sweat.

Useful Creativity

Reusing an old idea can make us feel lazy, shameful, or simply old. As a result, creativity has become a sacred cow. Leaders hold workshops to create new ideas, screen for candidates, respect creativity. But leaders too often create new things because they like the feeling and because they are ashamed of reusing old things. Leaders have an attachment to pride, and that attachment has unintended consequences.

After a heartbreaking loss in the 2011 Boston Marathon, Kenyan newcomer Sharon Cherop came to the 2012 race ready to win. Knowing that she could stay with the pack for most of the route, she planned her final sprint before the starting gun even fired. As tempting as it might have been to pull ahead after a water station or during the famous "Heartbreak Hill" section of the course, she stayed with the pack until the final moments of the race. As she rounded the corner that took her to the final 600 meters of the race, she sprinted the last leg, zooming ahead of the pack to take the top prize. Cherop champions the well-honed, perfectly timed surge. Relentlessly focused, she stayed on pace for 41,595 meters, and stepped on the gas for just 600.

Like Cherop, leaders must save their creative surge for the times when it's truly needed. Don't struggle to impress your people that you're a creative visionary. Take care of them and recognize their good ideas. The people you lead don't need a magic show to be reminded of how impressive you are.

In his 2002 memoir and master class *On Writing*, Stephen King urges aspiring writers to stop writing and start reading. Don't create, consume. Spend as much time as possible soaking up the work of others. Read while standing in line at the grocery store and with a flashlight after your spouse has turned out the light to go to sleep. If you want to write prose, read poetry. If you want to write genre novels, read literary fiction.[9]

Narcissistic creativity asks, "What can I create?" Useful creativity asks, "What does the organization need?" Useful creativity channels, sorts, repurposes, combines, analogizes, structures, and curates existing ideas. These are all ways to stay creative without inventing anything at all. Beware the bright and shiny new idea. Starting fresh feels good, but you may in the process abandon something that just required a polish or a tune-up.

Where does narcissistic creativity come from? I coached the head of an internal legal practice at a large company through a process to discover his source, and perhaps you'll recognize the same scenario in yourself or someone you work with. He said he should be doing a better job of soliciting the ideas of the people on his team. The top leaders at the company expected the legal team to do more than simply limit liability—they needed to support the company's business strategy. That meant rethinking the ways patents are registered and shared internally and externally, and it meant changing the nature of partnerships with law firms and regulatory bodies.

I asked the legal director why he wanted to be more accepting of others' ideas. An obvious question, perhaps. But I wanted him to articulate the value that supported the desire to include others. He said it was because he wanted to be a leader. But instead of accepting those new ideas, he killed them. He'd been trained to kill ideas from his work as a lawyer working with new ventures. Why was he killing those ideas? Because, he said, as a leader he felt the need to be the primary idea generator on the team. Several members of his team had made it clear they felt they were smart enough to have his job, so each meeting became an intellectual battle for the leader to prove his place. He was the boss because he was the best, and he needed to show it.

I found it refreshingly brave and honest for this successful corporate executive to admit to his need to be perceived as the most creative person on the team. He'd never voiced that desire before. Once he did, my job was largely done. He committed to experiment by surprising his team with support and encouragement at the next idea-generating session and to stop working so hard to prove that he was the only creative guru on the team.

Seven Ways to Make Your Creativity Useful

Eliminate the narcissistic creativity at work and replace it with some purposeful repurposing. Learn when thinking needs to happen inside the box and get better at receiving and using the bright ideas of others. As a leader, you need to create, and you need to help others create. Work to make sure all that creativity is useful.

1. Understand the Source of Your Creative Energy
The first step on the road to recovery from narcissistic creativity is to understand your own patterns of creative energy. Just as some people are morning people and others are night owls, everyone's creative energy has a natural flow, and if you've ever shared an office with an overly exuberant morning person you know that sometimes the energy can be a bit off-balance. If you take the time to discover your creative energy spikes, it's easier to manage them. In addition, it's important to know the source of the energy and your motivation behind it.

The urge to create can come from three places: pride, pressure, and boredom. The leader who creates something new out of pride is often new to a role, and he wants to make his mark. As he reshapes his team in his own image, needless changes ripple through an organization just so the proud leader can feel that he's made the place his own. A new house becomes your home once it feels, looks, and smells like your place. And the new leader naturally feels a desire to reshape an organization, even if things were just fine before he showed up.

Do you feel pressured to be creative just for the sake of creativity? If so, it's time to push back and make the case for some of the next six steps I describe. Some leaders celebrate creativity as a virtue so much that people feel they must generate something new. If your boss is in love with the idea of creativity, you have two choices. You can play along by reframing your old ideas in a way that feels sufficiently new. This is essentially tricking your boss, and I only recommend it if you've diagnosed your boss as hopelessly unable and unwilling to learn. The second choice is a tougher choice, but it's the leadership choice. Help your boss become more self-aware of her needless creativity. (I'd avoid using the word narcissistic with the boss.) And help the boss develop. "Managing up" — the act of pushing back and getting your boss to change behavior — is a good goal. "Leading up" — increasing your boss's long-term capability to lead — is an even better goal.

Finally, your urge to be creative could simply be boredom. When you take on a new role, you spend the first year riding up the learning curve and the second year mastering the role. If you've been in the same role for more than three years, it's natural to start to reinvent things just as a way to keep yourself engaged. I've worked with leaders who spent the early part of their careers moving quickly through many different roles, so their need for new challenges was naturally met. But left in the same role for several years, they crave a little novelty on the job, and as a result they change things that shouldn't be changed.

If you're familiar with the pressure to innovate but can't put your finger on a specific time you have personally over-created, is there a chance that you are putting this pressure on others? Are you yourself hesitant to let others approach problems without generating new solutions? Do you disproportionately reward members of your team who come up with new ideas rather than persisting with current solutions?

Until you are able to both identify the motivation behind the pressure to be creative and set yourself on a path to avoid the pitfalls of being too creative, too often, you will continue to produce ideas when you could save energy for when it is truly important.

2. Rechannel Your Creative Energy

Sarah recruits new volunteers for a large national nonprofit based in San Francisco. In college Sarah double majored in creative writing and graphic arts, and she typically has three creative side projects going at any time. As she describes it, sometimes her creative energy leaks into unhelpful places, such as redesigning a team process that works just fine. While Marcus Buckingham, the guru behind the strengths movement, would tell her that she'd be happier with a job that relied more on her strengths, for now she feels lucky to have a job in the city she loves. She's working toward a creative career, but her landlord insists on receiving a rent check every single month. So in the meantime she fights to stay focused on trusting the process of others and puts her energy into bringing top talent into the organization, not designing new systems.

When leaders like Sarah don't have tools to channel creative tendencies, even the tiniest of issues can be subject to the full innovation treatment, which dilutes the value of the solutions she can offer when the time is right.

Sarah should rechannel her energy. Keeping the solutions in proportion to the issues is the best way to stay on pace like the Kenyan marathoner, because if Sarah's not careful, she'll sprint on mile six with the burst of energy she gets from a water station and won't have enough energy to push in those final steps. Holding back creative energy for the times it's most needed requires self-control, especially for the most naturally creative thinkers. We expect marathoners to exhibit the discipline to hold on to a burst of energy for when it's most needed, but too often we hold creative types to a lower standard.

Rechanneling can often mean transforming that creative urge into a reframing of the problem. If it initially appears to need a whole new solution, can you take a step back and look at it with some new constraints? Sarah's new hires struggle with understanding the organizational structure during their first few weeks. Her first instinct, her creatively energetic instinct, is to swoop in and redesign the entire organizational onboarding system. The new hires need training and support. Every manager must own the onboarding process. Complicated process manuals need user-friendly one-pagers for new hires. Using the frames of creativity, her challenge looks like it needs a lot of new approaches.

Under the right circumstances, Sarah's region could probably use an improved onboarding system, but what she doesn't know is that in three months, she's going to need all of her creative energy to solve a major stakeholder buy-in issue. That's when she'll need to sprint, and she's about to use up all of her energy on what could easily be solved during the recruitment cycle.

A quick assessment of her energy spike leads Sarah to stop and reframe. "OK, there is a big information gap with our new hires. Where do we share the majority of information about any job?" Sarah quickly sees that there is a quick fix during the candidates' job interview: by including organizational structure as a component of the project, successful candidates will internalize information about organizational structure before they even arrive at their final interview. It's not a global solution, but it's much more reasonable than redesigning the entire onboarding process for new hires.

Sarah doesn't need to predict when she will have to flex her creative muscles. Instead, she needs to assess her current problem and determine if it deserves the full innovative treatment. That's the lesson here: if the problem *can* be solved more simply, it *should* be solved more simply. Reframing and asking the right questions can help a leader know when she should swing with the full weight of her creative hammer and when she just needs to give a little light tap of creativity.

For those of you with a big hammer of creativity in your toolbox, it can be a tough temptation to resist. You've probably been rewarded and praised for being so creative at work, and thus every vexing situation you face is another opportunity to reach for the hammer. But as a leader, consider when you need another tool. Maybe, for example, you need to borrow someone else's tool.

3. Repurpose on Purpose

To splash into the very crowded social media pool, tech innovators must not only stand out from the crowd, but they must have a truly unique idea. Right? Well, Ben Silbermann would likely disagree. Silbermann was obsessed with the idea of collections, beginning with his bug collection as a kid, and continuing into his adult life as he marveled at his friends' homes full of collections, from the mundane to the extraordinary. He and a friend left Google in 2008 with plans to build an app, and by 2009 they were well on their way to what would soon become one of the fastest-growing sites of 2012.

Silbermann's interest in collections quickly blossomed into the vision for Pinterest, an outstanding example of "repurposing on purpose." He took an ordinary idea—a pin board—and turned it into something extraordinary and, most important, easy to understand and use. Silbermann is a clever enough innovator to have created something wildly different from anything that has ever existed before, but instead, he repurposed something that users were already familiar with. Everyone knows the analog version of this—from placing things neatly in a box to cutting out pictures from magazines, humans like to collect and organize things, and Pinterest is a simple way to do this online.

Pinterest users can easily "repin" a post from anyone's collection that they like. Pinterest's success is built on the concept of repurposing; users see something they like, but categorize it in their own way, and others see it and get inspired for something else entirely. Just search for "mason jar" on Pinterest, and you'll start to see the scale of repurposing that Pinterest inspires in its users.

How can leaders imitate and repurpose like Silbermann? Well, just as Stephen King's suggestion for writers is to read, leaders must look at solutions that already exist. Ask yourself, who else has faced a similar

problem? Or what solutions to different problems could be begged, borrowed, and stolen for your purposes? If you are a leader of others, this
is the perfect opportunity to bring others into the solution space: many
minds searching for solutions are always better than one. Make it a mission and get everyone on board: everyone must find three creative solutions that someone else created for someone else's problem.

The act of borrowing thinking from someplace else takes a different
kind of effort. I work with an innovation professor who leads teams of
corporate executives through a process to develop new businesses. One
of the key steps in the process is to use analogies. He tells a few example
stories so the execs get the point. For example, a drugstore chain changed
the way pharmacists interact with patients to resemble the genius bar at
the Apple Store. Then he sets the groups going to think of analogies from
other industries that have faced and solved issues similar to the ones they
face. And, every single time, the conversation grinds to a halt.

The execs hate analogies. It seems irrelevant and a waste of time.
They want to get down to the real work of thinking about their specific markets and how to build a profitable, new business to serve those
markets. If the execs work for a company that makes power and automa-
tion products for a manufacturing context, then why should they waste
time thinking about another industry? They have deep expertise in their
industry, and only superficial knowledge of some other business. So with
a little bit of empathy and a lot of provocation, the innovation professor pushes the execs out of their comfort zone of experience. It's fun to
watch. The execs cling so tightly to their own world that it's a pretty tough
sell to get them to begin to embrace analogies as a business tool.

But once they do, the results are remarkable. It doesn't matter what
business you are in—there are more sources of innovation outside of
your industry than inside it. Break your problem down to the core
dilemma, then find world-class examples of attacking that core problem.
For example, Apple saw that technical expertise is too often hidden
behind a telephone bank. Yet it's expensive to offer live and in person.
At the Genius Bar at the Apple Store, you can get tech support live. This
is expensive for Apple, but people are willing to pay higher margins

for a product with that service. The pharmacy faces the same core challenge. Walmart is pushing the prices of prescription meds down, yet customers want a higher-touch service. The chain is redesigning its stores to make more pharmacists more accessible, and raising their prices in the process. It's a fundamentally different value proposition than the cheap, commoditized prescriptions from Walmart.

What's your core challenge? Strip away the industry-specific language. Are you trying to explain a complicated offering to a new segment? If so, check out Salesforce.com's use of simple language and images to explain cloud computing. They are the masters at conveying a very abstract concept in a clear, memorable way. What can you borrow from them? Are you trying to keep your best people from leaving to join faster growing start-ups? Look at how Chrysler kept its best engineers by including them in a challenge even bigger than starting something up — turning something around.

Sometimes you don't need a new idea, you just need to look for an old idea in a new place.

4. Make a Remix

Pablo Picasso was a master creator. From his first large oil painting at age fifteen until he died at ninety-one, he continued to produce art, most of it pushing the boundaries of genre and bleeding into politics and literature.

Picasso deserves the credit he gets for disrupting the art world at the dawn of the Cubist movement, dramatically overturning the long-held traditions of elitist portraiture and landscapes. Picasso wasn't creating something out of nothing, though. Cubism didn't spring forth fully formed out of his head, but was rather a smashup of conventional European portraits and the masks and art of tribal Africa. More than just an influence from previous genres, he was literally combining two old things into something very, very new. Travel to Picasso's native region of Andalusia, Spain, and you'll still find an eclectic mix of Arabic and Christian influences. Morocco is only ten miles across the Strait of Gibraltar from the southern coast of Andalusia. As he grew up, young Picasso was surrounded by a richly mixed bag of artistic and cultural influences from Arabic to Christian and African to European.

The heart of creativity lies in the new and successful combination of things previously uncombined. Here we can give our creative minds a break and our egos a rest, acknowledging that the best things are simply combinations of other things. Or, as Kirby Ferguson says, "everything is a remix."

Ferguson, a New York-based filmmaker, produced a series of compelling web videos that argue that virtually every piece of seemingly creative expression is a combination of pre-existing parts. As Ferguson reports in *Everything Is a Remix*, 74 of the top 100 films from 2002 to 2012 were either sequels, remakes, or adaptations. As he says, "transforming the old into the new is Hollywood's greatest talent." And to indicate how the transformation can become comically derivative, he points to *Transformers*, which includes "two sequels to a film that was adapted from an animated TV show based on a line of toys."

But where film critics might use this data to showcase how Hollywood has no creativity, Ferguson goes the other way. Hollywood has simply gotten really good at turning creative combination into a repeatable process. I used to look down on the derivative process of Hollywood because I wanted to believe in the heroic act of individual creativity. I'm not alone. In a *Fast Company* column in March 2007, the Heath Brothers show that the story of a company's creation morphs over time "to celebrate a flash of insight over stepwise improvements."[10] We want so badly to believe in the outrageous spark of genius that we bend our stories to reimagine creativity as a rare, heroic act.

But many innovations are simply inevitable consequences of time, bound to happen by someone, somewhere. As Kevin Kelly points out in *What Technology Wants*, over and over we see inventions happen at the same time around the world by people working completely independently. He points to the transistor created by Westinghouse in a Paris lab in 1948, the same year as Bell labs invented it in New Jersey. The ink-jet printer was created by HP, in California, and by Canon, in Japan, both in 1977. And in 1687 calculus was invented twice: once by Leibniz in Germany and once by Newton in England. Some might see coincidence but Kelly sees inevitability.[11]

Ferguson adds to the conversation of multiple discovery with a cinematic example. Charlie Kaufman's 2008 film *Synecdoche, New York* was described by the *Detroit News* as "A surreal exploration of art, love and death, it has the Felliniesque feel of some lost European cinematic masterpiece that reaches far past the normal boundaries of drama and into the very essence of existence."[12] So, hardly *Transformers*. But Ferguson shows how *Synecdoche* bears an "uncanny resemblance" to Tom McCarthy's 2007 novel *Remainder*. Ferguson never suggests that Kaufman stole from McCarthy—in fact, Kaufman's screenplay was written before McCarthy's book was published. But there was something inevitable about telling that story at that moment in time. "And actually, this," Ferguson continues to narrate in his own film *Everything Is a Remix*, "was written just before *The New Yorker* published a Malcolm Gladwell story. . . about the nature of innovation." The Gladwell article, "The Creation Myth," published in *The New Yorker* in May 2011, used many of the same examples that Ferguson does in his video. Meanwhile, the Heath Brothers column I referenced earlier, published in *Fast Company* in March 2007, was called: "The Myth About the Creation Myth." As Ferguson says, "We're all building with the same materials."

So free yourself from the burden of a blank sheet of paper and try instead to discover inevitable combinations. What can you remix at work? The basic elements of the creative process, according to Ferguson, are to "copy, transform and combine." I think that's a fine list, so I'll use it here. I suggest you start as I just did with step one: copy. If you weren't reading this book, what problem would you be solving at work? Who else has solved another version of that same problem? What can you copy from them? You'll transform the solution as you combine it with your own context in your own style. In fact, the sooner you start copying, the sooner you'll start making something new.

5. Create Analogies

When Greg Carroll, my former boss, took his role as vice president of marketing at Furman University, he told his team he wanted them to think of themselves as an ad agency. It's not uncommon for a small group of writers and designers inside a major corporation to think of themselves as an internal agency. But at Furman, this was a fairly radical act. The marketing staff at the liberal arts university in Greenville, South Carolina, were used to thinking of themselves as part of the "college relations" department. Even using the "M-Word," as Greg jokingly referred to marketing, was considered a bit edgy. The staff Greg inherited when he took over the job viewed their roles as writing and designing the alumni magazine, taking photographs of the stunningly beautiful campus, producing the internal newsletter, sending out press releases, and posting web pages. There was no unifying purpose or identity to the group besides working for Furman. They certainly didn't see themselves as part of an ad agency—most of them had never even walked inside an agency.

But for Greg, it was the perfect analogy to use. It aligned the group around a common cause and gave them permission to be experts in a way they had never been before. The group started to produce better work and they provided their internal clients with a higher level of service than before. Within a couple of years, applications were at an all-time high and the department won national awards for their website.

In the section on repurposing, I gave examples of strategic, corporate analogies such as learning to enter a new market from someone in a different industry. But as a leader, you can use analogies at a more local level. A good analogy will make people comfortable with the idea when you share it and help them understand. And it will also relieve the part of your brain that has to start from scratch with a solution. If you're trying to find a good analogy as a solution, try to first find one for your problem. Are you trying to increase internal stakeholder engagement in a structural reorganization? Who else has to get a lot of people on board for a change that will affect their everyday lives? How do they do it? How can you create an analogous experience so people not only understand the outcome, but also the process of how you will get there?

A lot of people congratulated us for our creativity when we created VVN. I was more than happy to accept the praise, but I felt a little bit guilty—we were, after all, only using what we had to create an experience people were familiar with. I was much more excited about Vivo Man before the event. We had the video technology, and people understood the structure of an interview, so why not just lead them there in a way they were comfortable with? It wasn't revolutionary, but the results were exactly what the client needed.

6. Fill Out the (Right) Form

A well-known CEO urged his marketing executives to be less creative. "You have an innovation muscle and an execution muscle. And most importantly, you have a brain that helps you know when to use which." The CEO was frustrated at wasteful innovation. In particular, he cited the example of multiple versions of marketing plans. He said the company needed to pick one. "We need a wide variety of good ideas, but a standard process for communicating internally. Can't we just pick a template and fill it out? Let's don't be innovative in deciding which template to use—let's be innovative in the ideas we put in those boxes."

Considering the overuse of the phrase "think outside the box," it's refreshing to hear the leader of a very innovative organization call for his people to spend some time inside the box. Recognize the significance of the frame and why it is there, and then execute with brilliance and even creativity within the frame itself.

The film industry can teach more about what it means to "fill out the form."

Blake Snyder's book on scriptwriting, *Save the Cat*, tells us that almost every successful script follows a fifteen-beat (plot point) structure, and deviating from this structure is akin to assuring your film will not get made, and if somehow it does, it will surely not be successful.

Think about two strikingly different films from 2010—*Winter's Bone* and *Toy Story 3*. Despite their differences, they both fit the structure of Snyder's "beat sheet."[13] From the opening shot that signals the central tension of the film to the moment all is lost, approximately 75 percent of the way through the movie, to the final image that demonstrates what our hero has learned through the journey, both films hit every beat. Another successful Hollywood script doctor,

Michael Hauge, insists that the one job of a movie is to elicit emotion, and, he argues, there are some fundamental steps that must be followed in order to elicit that emotion. Try to forge your own path to emotion and you will end up in the wilderness, lost and alone, with an audience as confused as the protagonist as to how you got there.

Opting to not fill out the form, or to create your own form—this is narcissistic creativity at its worst. We defined narcissism as an increased sense of self-importance, and just how important must you think you are to deviate from what's already working? The tighter the frame, the more impactful the changes are within it. Keep doing what's working, and your properly channeled creative energy will do the work for you. Our execution muscle, as the CEO implied, should be the big structural muscles that operate all the time, and when it's the rare and important time for innovation, you have specific muscles that are meant for that. The muscles we use for facial expressions are just as important as the ones we use for walking, but we wouldn't get anywhere if we tried to walk using our eyebrows.

As a leader, make sure you are filling out the right form. Make sure you've got the right box before you attempt to think outside of it. How can you inspire others to "fill out the form?" What can you do to find the right places to flex the creative muscle?

7. Curate

In a January 2011 article published by Jennifer Mueller, Shimul Melwani, and Jack Goncalo in Cornell's *Industrial & Labor Relations Review*, we learn that despite a constant narrative of the benefits of creative thinking, most people reject its output, creative ideas. They offer a solution: "if people have difficulty gaining acceptance for creative ideas, especially when more practical and unoriginal options are readily available, the field of creativity may need to shift its current focus from identifying how to generate more creative ideas to identifying how to help innovative institutions recognize and accept creativity."[14]

In other words, we don't need to become better creators of ideas, we need to become better curators of ideas. We learned to imitate and combine and analogize, but what if we aren't looking into the past for wisdom? What if the ideas come from your team or another department? Are you just as open to your coworker's ideas as you are to the innovations of Picasso?

Gallery curators are getting it right when it comes to being open to the ideas of others, and knowing how to "love on the art," rather than trying to operate in the creation space. If an artist had her own gallery and only showed her own art, she would likely have a hard time knowing what the best pieces were, or how to arrange the pieces in a way that tells a compelling story. Each piece is equally as valuable to an artist, so there must be others to help evaluate and put the art in the context of other pieces.

As a leader, you can think of yourself as a sort of "curator of ideas," holding them up to one another and finding ways to showcase the successes of others. Being someone who recognizes and appreciates good ideas is just as valuable as the curator who knows how to spot a potentially successful artist. Being a curator of ideas also supports the other steps to avoiding the sacred cow of creativity—a curator can sort, rechannel, imitate, combine, analogize, and fill out the form—because a curator is constantly in the presence of others' good ideas.

If you earn the reputation for being a leader who supports the ideas of others, you become a leader that people trust. Being a naysayer, no matter how outlandish or uncreative an idea, will not earn you the right to hear other ideas, which could be exactly what you or your organization needs. If you are truly asking the question, "What does my organization need from me?" the answer is not likely that it needs you to generate more and more ideas, but rather that you be a connoisseur of the best ideas out there.

Just as the best curators spend time with the art, spend time with the ideas. Put them next to other ideas. See what would happen if you turned it upside down or put it in a place all by itself. Does this idea fit with other ideas generated during a certain time, or does it belong in a genre of ideas created under a specific set of circumstances? How can you showcase this idea in a way that is less about the idea generator and more about the outcome of the idea?

Narcissistic creativity is obsessed with creating something out of nothing; necessary creativity curates the ideas of others. The pride you feel from showing off your one idea can be outmatched by the pride of artfully showcasing the ideas of many in a way that moves others to get on board.

Conclusion

It's natural to seek out new things. Some people have a special preference for novelty, and Robert Cloninger, a psychology professor at Washington University, has studied them. "Novelty-seeking is one of the traits that keeps you healthy and happy and fosters personality growth as you age," he told *The New York Times*.[15] "It can lead to antisocial behavior, but if you combine this adventurousness and curiosity with persistence and a sense that it's not all about you, then you get the kind of creativity that benefits society as a whole."

Cloninger provides an excellent summarizing definition of useful creativity. Stay adventurous and curious, but also stay focused on the business issue at hand. Combine your creativity with a healthy perspective so that the point of your creativity isn't self-aggrandizement but is in service of some larger purpose.

When you get the creative urge, pay close attention to the motivation behind your creative energy and put it to use where it belongs.

Putting It into Practice
WHAT IS USEFUL CREATIVITY?

Useful creativity is ideas and solutions created out of necessity, nearly always made up of previous thinking, that solve a problem as simply as possible. The key to honoring creativity as a value in the world of work is to keep it pragmatic and focused on the organization's needs—not on anyone's ego needs.

SO WHAT?

Creative leaders can be lured by their egos to present a new idea when an old idea will do just fine. There is a high value on ideas that come "out of nothing," when in fact, the best ideas are actually other versions of existing ideas. The energy it takes to constantly create drains fuel that leaders need to solve more pressing problems and decreases an organization's overall efficiency, effectiveness, and sense of stability.

NOW WHAT?

1. **Understand the Source of Your Creative Energy.** Consider the motivation for the need to create something new. Does the pressure come from a need to be praised or pressure to perform? Understanding the incentive makes it easier to avoid narcissistic creativity.

2. **Rechannel Your Creative Energy.** If you feel an urge to create something new, check yourself. Can you apply your creative energy instead to a more useful task, such as improving something that already exists?

3. **Repurpose on Purpose.** Beg, borrow, and steal from those who came before you and use an idea that already works for your own purposes. Remove the shame from emulating the best and support good use of good ideas.

4. **Make a Remix.** Take two unrelated things, smash them together, and see what happens.

5. **Create Analogies.** As you work to solve a problem at work, look to learn from a context that might seem on the surface to be completely foreign.

6. ***Fill Out the (Right) Form.*** Learn the underlying patterns for your work in the same way that screenwriters learn the classic beats of a screenplay.

7. ***Curate.*** Work harder on selecting, adopting, and displaying the ideas of others instead of creating your own work.

5

Process Outcome Excellence

Ella ran a team responsible for marketing a drug for a large pharma-ceutical company. Ella held herself and her team to the same high standards. She choreographed product launch events with the same relentless attention to detail that had driven her academic success. After earning a PhD in biology from Stanford and an MBA at Harvard, Ella had a long track record of striving for high standards. So Ella was shocked when her boss took her aside to tell her she was in danger of receiving a poor annual review. For the first few seconds of the conversation, all she could hear was the sound of her own heartbeat thumping in her chest. She replayed all of the sacrifices she had made for her job, and she was outraged. *What else did he want from her?*

"Ella, I think you thrive on intensity," her boss said. "But things aren't just intense on your team. They're tense."

As her pulse finally slowed, Ella realized that the one professional value she treasured most—excellence—had backfired. In school and in the early part of her career, Ella's obsession with producing the best work had always paid off. But something was broken now. Armed with this insight, Ella applied her well-developed "excellence muscle" to the new task of creating a more supportive culture and making it safer for her

95

team to ask for help. She started to listen more to her team and less to the relentless voice inside her head demanding that every action be perfect. Ella didn't need to lower her standards — she needed to raise her game.

High achievers like Ella sometimes obsess over excellence to the point of missing the bigger picture. Smart leaders understand that a maniacal focus on excellence can lead to blind obsession that lowers productivity and derails careers. But Ella was lucky enough to have a leader who helped her see her blind spot, and she was smart enough to learn to keep her high standards but broaden her perspective.

Inside the Secret Messiness of Excellence

If you ever need to kill someone's point in an argument, just whip out the mighty sword of excellence. It's the strongest weapon leaders have to win debates. "We need to protect our brand" is a nice way to frame it. Or if that doesn't work, blame someone else: "Our customers deserve better than this." Or invoke a higher power: "The CEO of this company won't accept lowering our standards, and neither will I." And if you need to buttress your argument with a pithy quote from a great leader, you have many to choose from. If you want to quote an American sports hero, use Vince Lombardi: "I will demand a commitment to excellence and to victory, and that is what life is all about."[1] If you prefer a military hero, choose Colin Powell: "If you are going to achieve excellence in big things, you develop the habit in little matters. Excellence is not an exception, it is a prevailing attitude."[2]

I especially detest the Colin Powell quote. Keep your desk neat, straighten your tie, practice your penmanship, and make sure you never make a suggestion that you can't support with rigorous data. Develop the habit of excellence in little matters. It's condescending advice that suggests you don't have the self-control to turn your excellence on and off. But too often it's advice that leaders have internalized because of the long, persistent campaign from experts who preach the value of excellence. If you work on an assembly line and want to keep working on that same assembly line for the rest of your life, I agree completely.

Show up on time and execute with excellence. As long as you're certain you'll never need to innovate or grow, focus on excellence in every single thing you do. Otherwise, you're going to have to get comfortable with a little bit of low quality from time to time.

My advice: be excellent occasionally. I doubt these words have been uttered by many head football coaches or four-star generals. But when we study leaders who accomplish great things, they seem to have a sixth sense that gives themselves permission to produce second-rate work on the way to doing a first-rate job. Often, the best leaders don't stop to think about their comfort with crap, and they certainly don't advertise it. They need their people to believe in their own ability to do great things. My goal in this chapter is to shine a spotlight on the best leaders' intrinsic ability to allow for occasional imperfections. How do you know when it's OK to lower your standards and still end up accomplishing great things?

Creating a tense environment as Ella did hurts workplace morale, reduces employee engagement, and decreases the chances of innovation and change. And excellence can backfire even for the leaders who don't have direct reports. Demanding excellence in every idea you share or rough draft you create is a recipe for aborting innovation before it has a chance to exist and grow into something meaningful. The easiest time to kill an idea is at its birth. And the easiest way to kill a weak, newborn idea is with the sharp blade of exacting standards.

Excellence not only kills ideas, it kills energy. When leaders demand perfection even in the unimportant details of their workday they waste emotional and intellectual energy, leaving less of their most precious resources for the work that matters most. Leaders too often demand excellence in the small things because they lack the will to prioritize what matters most. Love all your children the same, but don't love all your work the same. Some activities matter more and therefore merit more of your attention. Leaders must have the discipline and energy to make tough choices and give differently to different tasks. It's intellectually lazy to work hard at everything.

In Search of Excellence, by Tom Peters and Robert Waterman, is one of the most popular business books ever published. Peters and

Waterman urge leaders to raise their standards and produce excellence. They make no distinction between process or result, suggesting instead that excellence in everything leaders do is important. But Google famously launches rough works in progress and calls them beta versions. Tim Harford shows compelling research in *Adapt: Why Success Always Starts From Failure* that excellent outputs come from rough inputs in a trial-and-error process that favors the "just get started" mentality over a "make sure it's excellent" approach.[3] And Harvard Professor Clay Christensen, arguably the world's leading scholar on innovation, teaches the value of making mistakes early and adjusting.[4]

In the face of this movement in thinking, I imagined the authors of *In Search of Excellence* might have shifted their opinion. But as recently as August 2012, Tom Peters has stubbornly insisted on his point of view, taking to Twitter to spread the Gospel of Excellence. "There is one standard of Excellence," Peters (@tom_peters) tweeted. "Tiny invisible tasks command that standard as much as 'big' visible ones"[5] (Peters so admires the virtue of excellence that he capitalizes it). Peters isn't alone—he represents an ever-present call to raise quality, improve standards, and reduce errors.

When excellence in process is the mantra, there are unintended consequences. If you don't permit yourself—and your people—to explore and experiment, fail and learn, you slow down learning, which reduces the quality of the final output. Christensen in particular has done the research to reveal this paradox—relentlessly high standards can lead to a locked-in focus on providing your best customers with top-quality products, leaving a wide-open market for the scrappy upstart to disrupt.

I once observed the devastating unintended consequences of too much excellence process. In a conference room on the campus of a Big Global Tech Company (BGTC) a team of junior executives working in an action-learning project presented to an impatient senior executive. The junior execs had been asked to determine if the BGTC should launch one of its products in China. Everyone on the team had a flawless pedigree, with MBAs from top-tier business schools and experience at the biggest name investment banks or consulting firms before business school. The team was proud of their recommendation, but the senior executive rushed the team through the presentation deck they had prepared so carefully. When the team got to a chart labeled "Number of Libraries in China" the senior exec paused.

"Why is this chart blank?" he asked.

"Because," one of the junior execs spoke up, "we've been unable to determine at this point with any degree of certainty how many libraries are in China. Without that certainty, we didn't want to commit to a number."

Frustrated, the senior exec pushed the team to finally give a go/no-go decision. Should the BGTC launch its product in China?

"Based on the unavailability of the data regarding the number of libraries in China, we aren't able to offer a decisive point of view at this time," said another one of the earnest young execs.

"You mean you don't have a decision if we should launch in China?" said the senior leader.

"Because the number of libraries in China is quite important to our analysis, it would be imprudent at this time to make a decisive recommendation."

I don't remember exactly what the senior exec said in response, but I know it involved the phrase "we didn't get where we are today by being timid" and "have the guts to take make an educated guess and the sense to do a sensitivity analysis and move on." The junior team had been paralyzed by their need for excellence and certainty, and they'd hurt their reputation and slowed their company's progress.

A Second-Rate Path to a First-Rate Destination

After Bubba Watson won his first PGA Tour event, the Traveler's Championship in Connecticut, he shared his start to the game of golf with a reporter from the *Hartford Courant*: "I never had a [formal golf] lesson. My dad, he took me to the course when I was 6, just told me he was going to be in the woods looking for his ball, so take this 9-iron and beat it down the fairway."[6] As Watson was winning the 2012 Masters, Sir

Nick Faldo, a three-time winner of the tournament, described Watson's awkward, nontraditional swing. "It's not what you'd teach," said Faldo, "but it works." Faldo might question the excellence of Watson's swing, but he can't question the result.

Like Watson, Ed Catmull illustrates the desire for a relentlessly high standard in destination, but comfort in messiness along the way. Catmull cofounded Pixar and became the president of Disney Animation after Disney acquired Pixar. Many years before being acquired, Pixar signed a distribution deal with Disney that enabled them to get wide release for *Toy Story*, the smash hit that saved the company (before Disney signed the distribution deal that made *Toy Story* possible, Steve Jobs was in talks with Microsoft to sell Pixar to them). As part of the distribution deal, Disney asserted they had control over the sequel to *Toy Story*. Disney made sequels more cheaply and quickly than originals, and sent them straight to video, not to theaters. Under these terms, Pixar started down the path of making *Toy Story 2* as a subpar sequel when Ed and other leaders at Pixar, including *Toy Story* director John Lasseter, slammed on the brakes.

In a *Harvard Business Review* article and podcast, Catmull describes Pixar's unyielding dedication to hold each of their films to the same standard of quality. He tells the story of stopping other productions to make time to bring *Toy Story 2* up to their standards. Lasseter, in the documentary *The Pixar Story*, describes rewriting the film in one week-end. The new script demanded better special effects than the computer animators had ever created and it included a serious, slow ballad that explored the complex emotions of loss and abandonment. *Toy Story 2* would not be the trite, slapped-together sequel that had become the industry standard. "By rejecting mediocrity at great pain and personal sacrifice," Catmull said in the *Harvard Business Review* article, "we made a loud statement as a community that it was unacceptable to produce some good films and some mediocre films. As a result of *Toy Story 2*, it became deeply ingrained in our culture that everything we touch needs to be excellent."[7]

Sounds like Colin Powell, right? *Everything we touch needs to be excellent*. But look closer at the Pixar creative process and you'll find a cultural norm of sharing unfinished scene sketches and regular check-ins to review very rough work that may never turn into anything usable. It's a daily habit for these animators to show incomplete work to one another. By making it a norm, Pixar takes the sting of embarrassment out of the process. Each animator embraces the mess of progress, just as each one understands that there is no compromising on the quality of the finished product.

Leaders must tirelessly insist on excellence when it comes to the destination, but good-enough progress when it comes to the path. Catmull knows that to achieve excellence in the things that matter most, you need to create a safe environment. Excellence can be a noose that chokes off progress. Catmull makes it OK to share first-draft work.[8] And the best way to make it OK to share rough-draft work is to make it mandatory to share rough-draft work. Because every animator shares incomplete work every day, the messiness of progress becomes a norm that enables excellence in the outcome.

Leaders need a nimble mind to hold both those ideas at the same time. You must lower the day-to-day standards of work so that you can achieve the absolute highest standards at the end.

Seven Steps to Make Your Excellence Meaningful

These seven actions can help ensure that leaders are excellent at the things that really matter. This is an energy conservation program that preserves a leader's best for the most meaningful actions, and encourages a bit of play along the way. And it helps leaders create a culture that tolerates rough progress but insists on excellence in the end.

1. Lower the Stakes

The dumb jock is an old stereotype that persists. And in many cases, there is data to support the stereotype. Dropout rates are higher and grade point averages lower than the population-at-large for athletes recruited to colleges to play football and basketball. Thomas Dee, an economics professor at Swarthmore, wanted to understand more about the reason for the lower performance. More than eighty students at Swarthmore agreed to participate in the study. About half of them were on one of Swarthmore's NCAA sports teams. When the students signed up they were simply told they were taking part in an experiment to understand cognition. During the experiment the students were paid $15 to take a test. The questions were pulled from the GRE, the standardized test given to applicants to grad school.

Before they took the test, Dee primed some of the student athletes to get them thinking about themselves as an athlete. The primed student athletes were asked how much time they spent playing and practicing. The other student athletes were asked some dummy questions about how they got around campus. Priming is used to test the phenomenon of "stereotype threat." Claude Steele, the pioneer of this research, has shown that "where bad stereotypes about groups apply, members of these groups can fear being reduced to that stereotype."[9] Researchers have shown over and over that reminding people that they belong to a negatively stereotyped group can create anxiety that lowers performance.

And that's exactly what happened in Dee's experiment at Swarthmore. The athletes who were primed to think of themselves as athletes did fourteen percent worse on the test than the athletes who had been asked how to get around campus. Fourteen percent is a significant drop — the difference between a letter grade. That's a full point drop in GPA.[10]

When Emerald Archer was doing her PhD research at U.C. Santa Barbara she wanted to understand stereotype threat outside of a campus environment. She examined the stereotype that women perform worse than men in marksmanship exercises in the U.S. Marine Corps. She presented her findings in a paper called "You Shoot Like a Girl: Stereotype Threat and Marksmanship Performance in the U.S. Marine Corps."[11]

Shooting is core to the identity of a marine, and every marine must qualify on an M-16. Once again, the data supports the stereotype. On average, 68 percent of women qualify on their first attempt compared to

88 percent of men. And 23 percent of men are classified as experts, the highest level, while only 15 percent of female Marines attain that level. Archer wanted to know why.

She designed an experiment much more dramatic than the GRE test. Marines, both male and female, were invited to the rifle range to shoot a few rounds. They were told this was an experiment to test performance under a variety of conditions. All of the marines were given a page of written instructions before they started firing at targets at a distance of 300, 400, and 500 meters (more than a quarter of a mile!). On their instruction sheet, some of the marines were primed to think of the experiment as a test of the stereotype that women perform worse than men, while others weren't.

The stereotype threat effect held up on the rifle range as it had in the classroom. The female Marines primed to think that their gender was the subject of the test generally shot worse than the women who weren't primed to think that way. According to Archer, a female major said she felt added pressure on the rifle range because "she didn't want to be responsible for giving other female Marines a bad name."

But there was a surprise twist to the experiment that Archer didn't see coming. Half of the male Marines had also been primed to think of the experiment as a test of gender. So do you think the men primed to think of the experiment as a test of their dominance would perform better or worse than the men who weren't primed?

It turns out they performed worse. The prime had exactly the same effect on the men as the women. When women are told that men do better than women, anxiety lowers performance. Tell men the same thing and they seem to face the same anxiety, even though they're being reminded of their group's superiority. As Archer points out, "it is possible that the additional anxiety felt by male marines to confirm that they are indeed better than female marines led to their underperformance."

Leaders who are out to prove something on behalf of a larger cause create unneeded anxiety that lowers performance. When a young leader needs to prove to the world that he can present with as much confidence as his older counterpart, he creates anxiety that lowers performance. When an older executive feels the need to prove she can be just as innovative as her younger counterparts, she risks foolishly overreaching. The man who needs to show how male leaders can be compassionate or the female salesperson who needs to prove she can be as strong as any man creates unhealthy brain clutter that clogs up performance.

The first step for you to achieve excellence as a leader is to lower the stakes. Don't make everything you do a campaign for some larger group. If you want to hit the target, forget about the group you're a part of. Excellence is a tough aim to achieve without trying to change a stereotype along the way. Remove any priming that reminds you of your membership in some negatively stereotyped group and narrow your focus to the task at hand.

Do you want something you're working on to be really good? If so, ask yourself: Does it need to be good? Or are you just trying to prove that you need to be good? Is it about what the work needs, or what you need?

2. Ask Dumb Questions

Remembering you're in a group hurts performance. Remembering you're an expert also hurts performance, because expertise too often prevents you from asking dumb questions.

Phantom limb pain isn't just sad, it's weird. That's the way it looked to sixteen-year-old Katherine Bomkamp. She went to Walter Reed Hospital with her dad, a disabled Air Force Veteran. "There were all of these very young amputees returning from Iraq and Afghanistan, and they weren't a lot older than me at the time—maybe 18 or 19 years old," said Katherine. Always curious, Katherine got to know more about the amputees, and one of the first things she learned is that phantom limb pain strikes as many as 80 percent of amputees. The standard of care for phantom limb pain is often addictive painkilling barbiturates. But Katherine didn't know that. Her first thought: a heating pad. She used a heating pad whenever her leg hurt, and she figured heat might work for an amputee.[12]

Will a heating pad work on a prosthetic limb? That's a pretty dumb question. Where exactly do you put the pad? Then again, it's pretty dumb of the brain to think that its missing leg hurts. Katherine was naïve enough to think of the heating pad question. She wondered: can we trick the brain to think there's a heating pad on the limb? I love Katherine's thinking. *If an amputee's brain is dumb enough to be tricked into thinking it has an aching leg, can't we trick it into thinking that the aching leg has a heating pad on it?*

I don't know what you did for your tenth-grade science fair project. For mine I think I tested the effect of sunlight on flowers. Turns out it helps them grow. For Katherine's tenth-grade science fair project she built the "Pain Free Socket." In her own words, from the description she wrote when she was sixteen:

> Twenty-five feet of embedded thermo-resistive wiring is connected to a lithium-ion battery pack inside of a below-the-knee prosthetic socket . . . This treatment has the potential to be very effective as it takes into account the underlying factors producing the pain, does not use expensive (and largely ineffective) medications, holds no potential addiction factor, and has the ability to be produced in a portable and easily accessible environment.[13]

Katherine is now a college student and CEO applying for patents for the Pain Free Socket. Research scientists working on this problem for decades didn't think of her approach. Maybe a heating pad isn't an interesting therapy to consider when exploring the frontiers of medical knowledge. I'm sure the research scientists who didn't think of this idea have written many excellent grant applications and published a series of excellent articles in leading science journals.

If you need to *feel* smart you won't think of dumb questions. If you need to *look* smart you won't ask dumb questions. Both of those needs can get in the way of actually *doing* something smart. Expertise can be a curse. It's the sort of reward we work hard to achieve, and once having achieved it we must protect it. Like Gollum pursuing and then protecting his precious One Ring in *Lord of the Rings*, our desire to protect something often correlates with how hard it was to gain.

If you need to tackle that unhealthy desire to seem smart, hit it head on. Lead your team in a dumb-question lunch, where everybody asks the dumbest questions possible, with no eye-rolling allowed. As a leader you have a responsibility to create a safe place to experiment. That might mean clearing someone's calendar and it might mean clearing someone's conscience. Guilt can prevent playful exploration of new ideas and a sense of obligation can halt playful progress.

3. Embrace the Hacker Mentality

Denis Waitley, a motivational speaker and author of *The Psychology of Winning*, among other books, says that you should "take pride in your own efforts on a daily basis."[14] I disagree. Sometimes you should be ashamed of your work. Consider what Reid Hoffman, founder of LinkedIn, said at the South by Southwest Interactive Conference: "Launch early enough that you're embarrassed by your 1.0 product release."[15]

Mark Zuckerberg of Facebook conveyed the same idea in his first letter to investors as part of the company's IPO. In the letter, he celebrated the "hacker ethic," which has nothing to do with hacking in to people's private information illegally. "Instead of debating for days whether a new idea is possible or what the best way to build something is, hackers would rather just prototype something and see what works."[16]

Confronted with examples like this from the software industry, leaders who don't work in software have two options. They can say: *Sure that works for software. But we make real things with real consequences. We can't goof off like those kids*. Or leaders can say: *I wonder what we can learn from their world and apply in ours?* Encourage people to be embarrassed by the first version of the idea they share. Sell your people on the idea of living with some short-term shame in the name of long-term pride. This can be an important step in changing a culture from one that resists imperfection to one that makes it safe. You can't wave a magic wand and instantly create a Pixar-like culture in which it's safe to share incomplete work. Before it becomes safe, it might be a little shameful.

You're in a conference room listening to two people have the same debate for the sixth time. One says, "We've got to build this new system." The other one says, "Yeah, but people will never use the system once we build it." You could delay the debate by asking the two workers to gather evidence or check in with other people. Or you could kill the debate by challenging the person who advocates the new system to leave the meeting and test a prototype of the system that afternoon.

As the Old English proverb says, "the shortest answer is doing the thing."[17] (And there weren't many software companies in Old England.)

4. Accept the Mess of Progress

In 1999, when I worked as a communications instructor and the director of web development at Furman University, I had the idea to get several first-year students to post their experiences at college on the university's website. My goal was to increase applications, try out a new approach, and get free labor. I figured getting eighteen- and nineteen-year-olds talking directly to sixteen- and seventeen-year-olds would be more powerful than simply posting beautiful pictures and descriptions of the university. But the idea of giving the youngest students on campus control over part of the website seemed scary to some in the administration. With the support of a great boss and a very progressive administration, we built EngageFurman.com. The site wasn't part of the official furman .edu site, so we gave ourselves a little bit more freedom. Or, to be more accurate, we gave the students more freedom. I gave a few representative freshmen access to post their experiences on the site and a disposable film camera to document their first year. It was 1999, and digital cameras were still a little too expensive for us, so I processed the film at a local drugstore and scanned the photos. Blogging was new — I surely hadn't heard of it. But that's what we did. The university's marketing department didn't filter or censor what the students wrote, allowing them to speak directly to prospective students. (Since I was the only one with a scanner at the time, I did control what images were uploaded.)

The students wrote whatever they wanted to on the site. Sometimes they talked about their love for Furman, but other times they complained about the onslaught of tests, the clique-like feel of the Greek system, and the campus's somewhat remote location. As a result of the openness, the site got an instant credibility that no marketing copy could convey. Giving up control over the marketing message to teenagers took a bit of courage, but the risk paid off. By opening a direct, transparent communication channel between the teens attending Furman and the teens considering it, Furman got the sort of credibility that a slick marketing brochure could never achieve. Admissions went up, both in quantity and quality of applicants. Now it's commonplace for college admissions websites to have some sort of community that connects students with potential students.

Contrast Furman's student blogs with Wal-Mart's blogging experience seven years later. "Wal-Marting Across America" was presented as the actual, true journal of two friendly folks—Jim and Laura—as they drove across America visiting Wal-Mart locations. During their journey they checked in with many stores to find remarkable examples of community support and love. When it turned out that Wal-Mart's PR firm Edelman had paid for the whole trip and controlled the postings, *Business 2.0* magazine named "Wal-Marting Across America" one of 2006's "Dumbest Moments in Business."[18] Wal-Mart wanted the rustic, authentic populism of a blog, and they wanted to control their message. They wanted the credibility of a blog without the risk of bad PR. Instead, they got bad PR and no credibility.

If you're not prepared to pay the price of a mess you're not likely to get the benefit of progress. Progress is messy. Raise your tolerance for messes and you'll make more progress. To bring others with you, you'll need to share your mess, which can feel uncomfortable. But sharing a mess can be persuasive. As Baba Shiv, a professor at Stanford, said, "I have observed time after time that if you build a polished prototype others will see flaws. If you build a rough prototype, they will see potential."[19]

5. Start a Meaningful Journey with a Meaningless Map

In the harsh winter of the Swiss Alps, a Hungarian army troop on a training mission was stuck. The lieutenant in charge sent a small group of soldiers to scout the best way forward and return to the troop by nightfall with a recommendation on the best way back to the base. A snowstorm started soon after the scout team left, and the lieutenant wondered if he'd sent the scout team out on a suicide mission. By the second day when the scouts hadn't returned, the rest of the troop feared the worst. But on the third day the scouts made it back to join the troop and brought with them an incredible story of good fortune.

By the end of the second day, the scouts had become completely disoriented, with no agreement on which way to go to return to the troops. Then one of them found a map beneath their food supplies. The next morning they followed the map around mountains to make their way back to the troop. The lieutenant asked to see the map. "This isn't a map of the Alps. This is a map of the Pyrenees mountains 1,000 kilometers away!"

This story was first told by Hungarian Nobel Prize–winner Albert Szent-Gyorgi and was used by business professor and organizational psychologist Karl Weick to make the point that "if you're lost, any old map will do." As he says, "A map provides a place to start from, which often becomes secondary once an activity gets under way. Just as a map of the Pyrenees gets people moving so they can find their way out of the Alps, a map of the wrong competitor can get people talking so they find their way into the right niche."[20]

In *Flying Without a Net: Turn Fear of Change into Fuel for Success*, Tom DeLong shows leaders how to convert vulnerability and anxiety into strength. As part of his book, he diagnoses the way a love for excellence can stop people from even getting started. "The only way that you can change behavior," says Delong, "the only way that you can learn how to play golf, learn about algorithms, learn a new language, is that you're going to stumble and bumble at the very beginning. And that is the fear that so many of these high need for achievement personalities have, is that in that process, they're going to look bad, they're going to feel exposed, and they're going to feel silly. And that is what frightens them more than anything else—losing their image of competence."[21]

So stumble. Bumble. Get over yourself. Burnish your brand as a leader by taking some public risks, smartly. Leaders who must cling to an excellent map to get started may stay stuck out in the cold. Planning is a healthy process to get a team on the same page. But let your plan be a starting point, not a pair of handcuffs.

6. Embrace OK

In Allen Metcalf's book *OK: The Improbable Story of America's Greatest Word*, he reveals the power of OK, the most frequently uttered word on the planet and the first word said on the moon. OK has snuck from American English into languages around the world. Type OK into Google Translate and no matter if you select Danish, Filipino, Basque, or Russian, OK is translated the same way: "OK." OK was born in 1839 when a Boston newspaper editor playfully used it as an abbreviation for "Oll Korrect," which was his silly way to spell "All Correct." The paper's editor, Charles Gordon Green, used those sorts of silly abbreviations as a style that created a sense of in-group exclusivity for the readers who followed the paper closely enough to be in on the joke. But of all the silly abbreviations, only OK stuck. Why? According to Metcalf, "OK is the American philosophy, expressing in two letters our pragmatism, our efficiency, our concern to get things accomplished by hook or crook. We don't insist that everything be perfect; OK is good enough." Americans haven't just exported the word "OK" — they've exported the idea.[22]

The Hungarian scouts' map wasn't accurate. But, as it turns out, it was OK. OK might look bad compared to perfect, but it looks great compared to being stuck with nothing.

Leaders must encourage OK in themselves and others. One of the best leaders I've worked for let me be OK in a startling way. Blair Sheppard founded Duke Corporate Education in 2000 and was its CEO for eight years. He'd run custom executive education inside Duke's business school, and it was his idea to spin out of the school so corporate education could be centered more on clients' business needs instead of on faculty research agenda. As I mentioned earlier, it worked. Duke CE grew from about $12 million in revenue to about $60 million in revenue in those eight years and was rated as the best provider of corporate education in the world.

Blair and I traveled to Washington, D.C., to present to the CEO and the top HR executives of a defense contractor. We were bidding on a large leadership development program against several other elite providers. Our presentation went well, with Blair involving me equally, even though I had only a fraction of his experience and eloquence. During the Q&A, the CEO asked only one question: "How will we know if the program generates a return on our investment?"

I turned to Blair. I had heard him speak many times about measuring the ROI of leadership development. It was a topic he had a very clear, strong point of view on, and this issue was often what enabled us to win work over tough competitors. But Blair turned back to me. "Jake, you want to take that one?"

I swallowed hard and answered the question. I did fine, but not as well as Blair would have. We got the work, a long-term project worth millions of dollars. In the taxi on the way back to the airport, I asked Blair why he didn't feel the need to answer that question, CEO-to-CEO. "I wanted to show that we practice what we preach," said Blair. "We're suggesting to their leaders that they should push junior people to step up in moments of truth, so that's what I did. And besides, I knew you'd do OK."

It was a powerful act of leadership for Blair to let me know that he trusted that I would do OK. He resisted the urge to maximize excellence in that moment. But here's the paradox: by relaxing the standards in the short term, he raised the standards in the long term. My loyalty to him and to Duke CE has lasted for years because of the effect of moments like that.

Is there a war in your head, between the urge to develop your people and the desire to produce an excellent outcome? It's a natural dilemma of leadership. I suggest this is a time to remember bold balance and say yes to both of those options. Let your people feel the powerful motivational force that you trust them to be OK in the moments of truth and they'll worry as much about excellence as you. If they don't, then you've got the wrong person on your team, and you need to know that as soon as possible. Putting all the excellence on your own shoulders slows the development of your people and it prevents you from learning if they belong on your team.

7. Play Around

Reason magazine claims Norman Bourlag "saved more human lives than anyone in history" by starting the Green Revolution that boosted wheat production in Mexico, Pakistan, and India.[23] Bourlag was a scientist who studied plant pathology at the University of Minnesota and later developed and advocated high-yield grain for areas with exploding population. Bourlag won the Nobel Peace Prize.

There are many grand things to learn from Bourlag about innovation and determination, but my favorite lesson is the value of getting out of the lab to start making things happen in the field. When Bourlag described his initial efforts to get Mexican farmers to use a new variety of high-yield wheat seed, he said: "The farmer won't do this if it's done on an experiment station, because he can't tell how much science and technology went into that and how much witchcraft. But if it's done on his own land, if he participates in putting in this demonstration, and if you provoke this big increase in yield, then he's very receptive."[24]

A collaborative demonstration on a farmer's own field is messier and dirtier and less likely to produce the pristine results of a demo on an experiment station, but it's much less likely to feel like witchcraft.

For many scientists, the job of an experiment is clear: help answer an unanswered question. Whether it's a clinical trial of a drug, a rifle range test to understand the impact of stereotypes, or a test of new wheat seeds, experiments exist to help scientists figure things out. But Bourlag wanted to do more than answer questions. He got out of the lab and lost some of the pristine scientific rigor of a controlled experiment in order to gain traction in the real world.

Scientists in social and medical research often need subjects to take part in their research. People participate in experiments for a small fee or just because it feels good to help the cause of science. But the people aren't the point; they're the human lab rats serving the needs of the scientists.

Just as Bourlag challenged traditional tenets of science, Beck Tench is rethinking the purpose of a research subject. As the director for Innovation and Digital Engagement at the Museum of Life and Science in Durham, North Carolina, Tench started "Experimonth," a new approach to science in which the subjects, not the scientists, are the heroes. Anyone who's interested can sign up for a month-long experiment designed to address a topic of interest to researchers. For example, the April 2011 Experimonth studied mood. One hundred seventy-two people signed up and agreed to receive five text messages a day asking to rate their current mood on a scale of 1 to 10. The research revealed some interesting findings. Mood was lowest on Mondays, it grew slowly during the week until it peaked on Sunday, and then it dropped back down on Monday. Women rated their moods slightly higher than men. Mood was lowest at the start of the day, rising gradually throughout the day. And there were slightly wider swings in mood for older participants than for younger ones.

The findings were interesting, but here's what got the attention of scientists around the world: the compliance rate for Experimonth was 81 percent. For a month-long project that required participants to send five data points per day, that's extraordinarily high.

Tench isn't a scientist by training. But when she reported the results with the participant compliance, several scientists got in touch to ask how she had achieved such a high participation rate. Tench told them that the entire experiment was designed around the needs of the research subjects, not the needs of scientists. She graphed the total results of the group in real time so the participants could see where they stood compared with the group. And there was no control group held out of the study—everybody who participated had their data included.

What motivated people to stick with the study? It offered an easy, immediate way for them to get meaningful, personal insight that helped them see how they compared to a group. We can look around the world and see how our looks fit in or not, but it's difficult to know how we *feel* compared to others. In short, it worked because it was fun.

Tench sacrificed some of the scientific integrity of the study (no control group) to make it more meaningful for all of the participants. To her, the job of an experiment isn't simply to help scientists know things. Experiments help get more people excited about knowing more things about themselves and the world. She's one of the leading proponents of citizen science, a new approach to get more people involved in more science.

And there's a surprise twist to the story of citizen science. The tradeoff—get more people involved but give up on statistical reliability—doesn't always happen. Laura Germine, a postdoc at Harvard's Psychology Department, did tests to compare the reliability and integrity of data that came from online volunteers versus the traditional approach of paid test subjects in a lab. She found that the tradeoff doesn't exist, at least not nearly to the extent that scientists had feared. As she puts it, using the Web to gather data from volunteers is "fast, it's cheap, but it's not dirty. In experiments like ours, what you're getting is good, reliable data."[25]

If scientists can permit themselves to challenge some of the sacred cows of process, surely leaders can find a scratch pad. Create a workplace environment that is appropriately playful. Lighten the mood and learn new perspectives in the process. Plato said, "You can learn more about a person in an hour of play than in a year of conversation." So get to know your teams better through playful experiments.

A final note: I'm not talking about occasional trips to the golf course or go-kart racing as a relief from the drudgery of the job. I'm suggesting that work itself should involve less drudgery and should feel more like racing go-karts. And don't think playing is the province of unproductive children. As the very productive playwright George Bernard Shaw said, "We don't stop playing because we grow old, we grow old because we stop playing."

Conclusion

The 2012 Grammy winner for best orchestral performance was Gustavo Dudamel, who won for conducting the Los Angeles Philharmonic's performance of Brahms's Symphony Number Four. Dudamel became the music director of the L.A. Philharmonic three years earlier, when he was twenty-eight years old. Perhaps the most famous music conductor in the world, *60 Minutes* called him "the next Leonard Bernstein."[26] Born and raised in Barquisimeto, Venezuela, Dudamel is a product of *El Sistema*, the program that gives children throughout the country the opportunity to play music at an elite level. Dudamel isn't alone. The Simon Bolivar Symphony Orchestra (SBSO) of Venezuela tours the world and was called by *The London Times* one of the five best orchestras in the world. Jose Antonia Abreu founded *El Sistema* in 1975, and he was awarded the TED Prize in 2009 for his achievements. Surely this is mastery and excellence at the highest levels.

Alejandro Carreño, the twenty-seven-year-old concertmaster of the SBSO, says that it doesn't start out that way. "For most orchestras around the world," said Carreño, "you master your instrument first, then you join the orchestra. But here it's exactly the opposite. With *El Sistema*, every kid who wants to play is invited to join a local orchestra that is part of the system. And from there, we master our instruments together."[27] Taking music from the elite few and giving it to the masses is messy. There might be noise along the way, but there's music at the end.

When leaders tolerate more playful experimentation on the path to a destination defined by excellence, they increase the chances that people will stay engaged and produce truly distinguished work. Sometimes the progress may be lower than the normal standards have been, and that can lead to the very difficult decision to share work a leader isn't proud of. But so long as a leader is OK with the mess of progress, the final result can be a masterpiece.

Putting It into Practice
WHAT IS OUTCOME EXCELLENCE?

Outcome excellence is demanding high standards in setting important, macro goals, instead of a micro-focus on perfection in each step along the way. The key to honoring excellence as a value in the world of work is to know when to seek it, and to give yourself and your people permission to play, fumble, and create second-rate work in the service of doing a first-rate job.

SO WHAT?

Excellence becomes a sacred cow when it's used reflexively instead of purposefully. Leaders need to purposefully embrace low quality when it's smart, while aiming for excellence in the ultimate objective they shoot for.

NOW WHAT?

1. **Lower the Stakes.** Don't burden yourself by viewing everything you do at work as a referendum on how qualified you are to hold your current position. Instead reduce the emotional load of work by adopting a shorter-term perspective.

2. **Ask Dumb Questions.** Become an expert at forgetting the orthodoxies and accepted truths related to your work. Make it safe for others to question basic principles instead of feeling the need to demonstrate expertise.

3. **Embrace the Hacker Mentality.** It's OK to feel a little shame and discomfort with your work — it can be a sign that you're taking the risk of getting your ideas to market more quickly. Let go of the need to feel pride in everything you do and you'll end up with more work to be proud of.

4. **Accept the Mess of Progress.** Make it a habit for you and your people to share incomplete work as a way to create a culture in which people feel safe producing the low-quality work that needs to be created on the way to excellence.

5. **Start a Meaningful Journey with a Meaningless Map.** Start making progress towards excellence today. Any plan will do the job of getting you started. Adjust your route while you're moving.

6. ***Embrace OK.*** As a leader, it's important that you create a climate of acceptance and tolerance. Perfectionism crowds out completion, preventing the team from advancing toward important, ambitious outcomes.

7. ***Play Around.*** Once you've created a sense of purpose for yourself and your team and a climate of acceptance, lead short bursts of fun, playful exploration.

6

Outcome Process Fairness

As the head nurse in the intensive care unit, April manages a team of seven registered nurses at a hospital in rural Georgia. One of her employees, Leah, is an all-star performer who can be relied on to carry out her duties professionally, with good humor and good results. Each of April's other employees has at least one weakness she's coaching them on, ranging from poor punctuality to workplace drama. But Leah stands out.

Last year April sent Leah to a training program in Orlando that was important for her development and a nice fringe benefit that rewarded her hard work. Leah took her husband with her and enjoyed the days off and complimentary hotel stay. This year there's a new training opportunity in Myrtle Beach, and once again April only has the travel budget to send one person. Although she believes that Leah—and her unit—would benefit most from sending her for the second year in a row, she feels her team would find that to be unfair. April doesn't want to deal with the complaints and accusations that Leah is her favorite, so she sends one of the average performers to Orlando.

Miffed at her boss's gutless act, Leah uses her good reputation to take a new role in a different unit in the hospital. Now April is left with her weakest employees and the need to hire someone fast. She aimed for fairness, but it backfired.

April was right to worry about creating a fair work environment. If the process for deciding rewards and recognition is unfair, workers will lose their motivation. But April was wrong to let her desire for fairness bleed over into a concern for fair outcome. Fairness becomes a sacred cow at work when leaders obsess over fairness of outcome, instead of setting up a fair process and letting the chips fall where they may.

Fair Minded

Economists, neuroscientists, psychologists, and even mathematicians agree — we humans want desperately to live in a fair world. Neuroscience research shows that the instinct to treat each other fairly comes from deep within our psyche. In one dramatic experiment, two people were strapped into two different MRI scanners within sight of each other in the same room. When one of the participants was given a painful shock, the MRI scan showed the other person's brain experienced many of the same effects. Quite literally, we feel each other's pain.[1] And we feel each other's pleasure. Other MRI studies have shown the reward network in our brain is activated when we see people treated fairly.[2] Giving someone else fair treatment gives our own brain pleasure.

Experiments and research over the past twenty years have shown that economists had it wrong. Economists had claimed we humans are rational self-actors seeking only to maximize our own interest. Instead, we will pay to make sure we live in a fair world, even if it means hurting our own situation. We'll give up money to reward someone whose made a sacrifice to help others. And we'll spend our own cash in order to punish someone who has taken more than their fair share. Matthew Rabin, who teaches at U.C. Berkeley, is the pioneer of the study of the "Economics of Fairness" and is perhaps the preeminent scholar in this area.[3] Economics is often called the dismal science because it assumes the worst intentions in all of us, but Professor Rabin and friends show us that we aren't all that dismal.

Psychologists have studied nonhuman primates, like chimpanzees, to learn how empathy—our desire to treat others fairly—is connected to something more primal even than humanity. As Frans De Waal says in his outstanding book *The Age of Empathy*: "We involuntarily enter the bodies of those around us so that their movements and emotions echo within us as if they're our own."[4] Have you ever fed a baby a spoon of baby food? As you watched the baby chew, did you find yourself pantomiming the chewing motions of the baby? This sort of mirroring, or "body mapping" as De Waal calls it, is a deeply human instinct that reveals something poignant and important about our deep instincts for social connection and empathy. Isn't it nice to learn that empathy is such a natural act? It's a gift we're born with.

In *Why Beauty Is Truth: The History of Symmetry* mathematician Ian Stewart shows how and why nature loves symmetry as much as primates love fairness. From a butterfly's wings to the supersymmetries of string theory, balance abounds.[5] And what is fairness, except our own human nature striving for symmetry? When you treat me as I treat you, it feels fair. When what I give equals what I receive, it feels fair. Fairness is symmetry applied to human nature.

We yearn for fairness because we are biologically programmed to do so. But fairness doesn't just spring forth from within us. Politicians call on us to rely on the "better angels" of our human nature—Abraham Lincoln was the first to use this phrase. Sports writers and coaches celebrate athletes who put the team before the individual. This is the "secret" at the heart of Bill Simmons's best-selling *Book of Basketball*.

We deify the heroes of film who sacrifice something of themselves for a larger cause, while we demonize the villains who selfishly worry about their own needs first. Stanley Williams, author of *The Moral Premise*, used his Ph.D. research to show that the more frequently and clearly a film conveys a theme that truth triumphs over wickedness, the more money the movie makes at the box office.[6] Fairness is within us and around us. Scientists teach us that fairness works like a drug.

We mean well, we want to be fair, and we try to help others. Yet too often we project our needs onto others. Once we've projected those needs onto someone else, we work hard to satisfy them. And it feels good to our brains, like a drug. Feeling fairness activates the reward network in our brain. Even when we haven't actually met someone else's needs, as long as our brain feels that good intention it's happy.

The first side effect of fairness is self-focus. The pursuit of fairness may cause you to treat others the way you want to be treated, without taking the time to discover if their needs are different from yours. Our brain's reward network needs help. By training your brain to question the voice that says, "Good job, you helped someone out," you give your prefrontal cortex a much-needed workout. Left unregulated, our brain is wired to give others the gifts we want.

As with many aspects of the human condition, this phenomenon was beautifully demonstrated by *The Simpsons*. In the episode "Life on the Fast Lane," which won the 1990 Emmy for Outstanding Animated Program, Homer gave his wife Marge a bowling ball for Christmas. When Marge reminded Homer that she didn't bowl, Homer helpfully suggested that he could use it. In fact, in anticipation of Marge rejecting the gift, Homer had his name engraved on the ball. Homer, as is often the case, epitomizes the unregulated part of the adult brain acting only on its base urges. The point: sometimes, like Homer, we give the gifts that we want to receive.

Consider the manager who rewards her hardest working employee with public recognition, like a giant blue ribbon on the lucky winner's cubicle. Enlightened management, right? It saves the company money (blue ribbons are cheap), meets the intrinsic needs of the person being recognized, and encourages others to follow in the lucky person's footsteps. But here's the problem: not everyone feels the same way about attention. I've seen this sort of recognition lauded and taught by managers. Maybe the boss would love a big blue ribbon on her office door. So she assumes that giving recognition to others is a gracious act of leadership. But depending on culture and personality, some folks feel embarrassed by being publicly called out. Maybe the hard-working employee would appreciate a heartfelt thank-you in private much more than a garish display. Some folks love the attention. The point is, the boss can't assume.

Fairness doesn't merely trick you into thinking everyone wants what you want. It can also trick you into making some poor decisions. These decisions, demonstrated in a powerful piece of research carried out as a game, feel good to you even as you cause yourself to suffer.

Fehr Game

One of the leading thinkers in the world of fairness and spite is Ernst Fehr, an Austrian economist who teaches at the University of Zurich in Switzerland. Fehr (whose name is pronounced, coincidentally, "fair") uses games to discover how far people are willing to go to arrive at a fair outcome. One of the most interesting of the experiments he created is called the third-party punishment game.[7] In the game, there are three players: A, B, and C. To make this easier to follow, let's give these characters names. We'll call the three people Alice, Bob, and you — you play C. At the start, Alice gets $100, Bob gets nothing, and you get $50. When you agreed to participate, you had no idea what to expect. Now you're holding five, crisp ten-dollar bills in a small, poorly lit conference room in the psychology building, with an earnest grad student running the experiment.

The game begins when the grad student asks Alice to decide how much of her $100 to give to poor Bob, who has nothing. She can decide to give Bob nothing, or everything, or any amount between $0 and $100. No one is allowed to attempt to influence Alice in any way — not Bob and not you. After Alice decides how much to give, things get interesting. The grad student turns to you and tells you that if you think Alice was unfair, you can punish her, but at a price. You can use some of your $50 to reduce the amount Alice gets. For every dollar you spend, you reduce Alice's take by three dollars. But nothing you do will affect the amount Bob gets — Alice was in complete control of that decision. And now you're in control of this one.

Imagine Alice decides to give Bob a mere $30 and pocket $70 for herself. And imagine this makes you mad. So you decide to punish Alice and reduce her take by $30, just to make things a bit more even. To do this, you have to spend $10 of your own money. As a result, now Alice ends up with $40 ($70 – $30), Bob still ends up with $30 (you can't help Bob in this experiment, you can only hurt Alice), and you end up with $40 ($50 minus the $10 you just spent to punish Alice).

Was your decision smart? You certainly didn't maximize your take. Was it fair? On the one hand, you acted in the best interests of others. But who are those others? Remember, you didn't help Bob. You just punished Alice. Maybe you tell yourself that you taught Alice an important lesson and helped protect other people in the future, in case Alice ever does this exact experiment again. We tell ourselves a lot of strange things to make spite seem nobler. The truth is, you just lost $10 you could have spent on yourself or a loved one.

Fehr's experiments illustrate how the punisher, no matter who they are or where they live, will consistently give up money in order to punish any selfish player. We want fairness so badly that we will sacrifice just to make an unfair player suffer a bit. It's like the story about me missing my daughter Clara's birthday from Chapter One: she was willing to give up the chance to get a nice present just so that Emily would be forced to miss out on her birthday with Dad. And by the way, the results of the experiment have been validated across culture, age, and gender. So it's not only nine-year-old girls who engage in this behavior. In an attempt to live in a fair world, you may put your energy into bringing others down to your level instead of bringing yourself up.

Seven Ways to Train Your Brain to Focus on Process Fairness

Well-intended effort to ensure a fair outcome can increase spiteful score-keeping behavior, reduce the differentiation and meaningfulness of rewards and recognition, and enable ethically questionable decisions. The line between process and outcome fairness can be a slippery one.

Your brain may have spent decades seeing the world in a general haze of fairness. Sharpen up your thinking and avoid tripping up on the carpet snag of well-meaning or ill-conceived fairness.

1. Projection Detection

Think of the people at work you need to influence: your employees, your boss, your clients, executives, customers, suppliers, bankers, or anyone else whose opinion or behavior you'd like to shift at some point. Are you able to clearly articulate how their motivation differs from yours? Do you believe that "everyone really just wants money" or "everyone really just wants some recognition" or "everyone just wants to know where they stand" or "everyone really just wants" *anything*?

In the case of the manager looking to motivate her employees, she's got to take the time to learn that not everyone needs what she needs. Instead of empathizing, she needs to do a bit of discovery. Left unchecked, our empathy can become our enemy.

You may be giving away things you don't need to give away, wasting time and resources. Team leaders fall easily into the trap of self-focus, motivating their employees the way they themselves would like to be motivated. As a result, the team becomes disengaged and the team leader becomes frustrated.

Despite your best intentions, do you, like Homer Simpson, give the gifts you want to receive? Have you projected your own wants and needs onto others? It's a normal mistake for the voice in your head to make, until it's been properly trained.

I recommend a simple, three-step process as the antidote to the self-focus side effect:

1. Know your needs and wants
2. Know the needs and wants of others
3. Look for the differences between 1 and 2

The trick here is to have enough self-awareness to know the things that you would want if you were in the other person's shoes, the patience to get to know what the other person *actually* wants, and the discipline to see the difference between the two. Think of this as the self-focus serenity prayer. It's much more helpful at work than the Golden Rule, which assumes that others want what you want.

2. Break the Golden Rule

Paul Zak's research is both wildly divergent and narrowly focused. On the one hand, Zak's work crosses boundaries and disciplines. He's a professor of economics, psychology, and management at Claremont Graduate University, and he's a professor of neurology at Loma Linda University Medical Center — both in Southern California. And yet across this diverse academic path he's focused for the past decade on the effects of a single molecule — oxytocin. The brain's signal to a woman's body to start producing milk for her newborn, oxytocin's powerful effects are only now being fully understood across men and women. In his book *The Moral Molecule* Zak explains that "oxytocin generates the empathy that drives moral behavior, which inspires trust, which causes the release of more oxytocin, which creates more empathy." Despite the deep scientific research behind his work, Zak promotes oxytocin with the zeal of an infomercial host hawking a weight-loss pill. "When oxytocin surges," he writes, "people behave in ways that are kinder, more generous, more cooperative, and more caring."[8]

But not surprisingly, I'm curious about the unintended consequences of oxytocin. According to Zak, this molecule drives the human virtue to do unto others as you would have done to you. The Golden Rule. Of course, the problem with the Golden Rule is that not everybody wants done to them what you want done to you. Surging oxytocin triggers the release of the neurotransmitters dopamine — which makes us feel happy — and serotonin — which makes us feel calm, so the Golden Rule can be a really tough rule to break. We have a strong biological payoff to help others by giving them stuff that we think they want because we want it.

Working with a group of executives at another big, global needs-to-be-nameless company, I witnessed the powerful tug of self-focus and the anxiety that can come with breaking the Golden Rule. An executive — let's call her Carolyn — shared a story. Carolyn oversaw a team of managers, each of whom led a small team of software developers. One of the young, star developers — call him Tom — two levels down from Carolyn had been identified as a flight risk because he'd received an attractive offer from a start-up that the big company couldn't match. Tom's boss, "Sharon," reported to Carolyn.

Carolyn was careful to give Sharon autonomy as she worked on keeping Tom in the company. Carolyn hated to be micromanaged and so she was careful not to make that mistake. She didn't need to tell Sharon that it was important to keep Tom. It would be patronizing for Carolyn to point out such an obvious fact. No one knew more about Tom's importance than Sharon. Carolyn detested it when her own boss pointed out the obvious, as if she weren't smart enough to figure things out herself, so she gave Sharon exactly the same respect and space that she would like to get. It probably felt really good to Carolyn to give Sharon something that Carolyn wanted but never got. To Carolyn, nothing was more motivational than autonomy.

But the autonomy backfired. When Sharon came in to Carolyn's office to report that Tom was leaving to join the start-up, she added a surprise twist. Sharon was leaving too.

"This can't be too much of a surprise, Carolyn," said Sharon. "And I doubt it's much of a disappointment. You never seemed too worried about the possibility of losing us."

What felt like autonomy to Carolyn felt like abandonment to Sharon. As Carolyn told the story, she revealed her own uncomfortable truth. She believed that "real leadership" was her kind of leadership. But now she felt that she needed to grow as a leader, to flex into different styles of leadership.

"As it turns out," she said in a leadership workshop, "I realized that Sharon was a more mature leader than I was. She welcomed help and input, while I felt the need to prove my worth through my own individual efforts. This was a very painful way to learn the lesson. I needed to give her the leadership she wanted, not the leadership I wanted to give."

Situational Leadership™ is one of the oldest—and wisest—lessons in the leadership canon. The point is elegant and simple—a good leader diagnoses a situation, and, depending on the context, provides a different leadership style. Here's how fairness and the side effect of self-focus connects to Situational Leadership: sometimes our ability to pivot to a style is slowed down because we cling to our own preferences. We give the leadership style we want to receive, instead of giving the leadership that will provide the greatest effect.

3. Vive la Différence!

Sameness is the second way fairness backfires. Self-focus means assuming others want what you want, whereas sameness means lumping everyone together in the same big bucket of need. It means treating everyone in a group the same, even if they each need some very different treatment.

When April—the manager who sent her second best nurse to Myrtle Beach—focused on what she thought was fair, she suffered from sameness. We don't just treat people the same because we're lazy; we treat people the same because we want to be fair. With so much pressure to be fair from inside us and around us, it's no wonder.

Consider a university president who felt it no longer made sense to fund a celebrity-packed jazz festival for the university's highly regarded jazz program. Most departments at the school struggled to fund basic curriculum. It hardly seemed fair to allocate precious resources to the healthiest department for an event with only a thin educational purpose.

So the president canceled the festival. As a result, the jazz program—the university's highest-profile program—struggled, alumni pride took a hit, and alumni giving dropped, leading to a deeper range of cuts and layoffs throughout the university.

Did the president make a fair decision? Yes. But did he make a smart decision? I don't think so. Instead of the discretion, courage, and communication skills needed to make and execute a tough decision at a tough time, he defaulted to fairness.

For another example of the sameness side effect, consider upscale hotels. The Ritz-Carlton Hotel prescribes exactly the formal greetings its staff should use when greeting guests ("How might I help you, Sir?") and exactly how far away they should be when greeting a guest (ten feet). The Four Seasons simply asks its staff to make their guests feel at home. No loyalty cards or customer profiles; just human, in-the-moment connection. The Ritz has more sameness, while the Four Seasons has higher customer satisfaction and a growing market share.

In their book *Best Face Forward*, Bernie Jaworski and Jeff Rayport from Monitor Consulting tell the Ritz-Carlton story and others related to outstanding customer service. They conclude that the keys are: hire great people, make sure they understand the company's strategy and believe in the values, then get out of their way and trust them to exercise their judgment in the moment. It's difference that delights, not fairness.[9]

Leaders at a global software company missed this lesson. They worked with small, local businesses to deliver solutions to clients built around their company's software products. In Texas the company relies on three of these local business partners to do work with banking clients. Someone inside the company complained that a fourth partner, who hadn't worked in the industry, deserved a shot at these deals, even though the three primary businesses have never disappointed. So the fourth partner company got a chance, performed poorly on an implementation deal, and lost the account. Fooled by fairness again.

If you ask the people who made the decision, they'll tell you this wasn't about fairness at all. It was about building depth, growing the ecosystem of partners, deepening the bench, blah, blah, and blah. This is called rationalization. We humans tend to make decisions based on emotion — in this case, because fairness feels good — and then justify those decisions with smart-sounding, rational arguments.

Instead of treating a group of people fairly, you may simply treat them each the same. But fairness does not equal sameness.

4. Discriminate Courageously

To cure sameness, I recommend we learn from marketers and embrace the power of differentiation. The marketing geniuses at Coke treated me differently. They knew that I was finally ready to embrace a diet version of my favorite carbonated beverage, but they also knew that Diet Coke didn't feel right to me. It felt like something my Mom drinks, which is exactly what their research predicted. So Coke created Coke Zero and marketed it with some hip, self-deprecating commercials aimed at men younger than 45.[10] And now I have the brand I need to step fully into the world of diet soda. They made me—and the millions of others who belong to my demographic group—feel special.

In the world of mass marketing, differentiation involves market research and creativity. To apply the lesson from Coke to the treatment of individuals you don't need research. You need a little bit of courage and a lot of communication skills.

Explaining to your direct reports why you'll be sending the same person to the training trip for the second year in a row takes sensitivity and guts. Making the case to continue to invest in one department at the expense of others requires world-class influence skills. Depending on the latest business jargon, these are either "difficult conversations," "fierce conversations," or "crucial conversations." Whatever you call them, you need to be able to have them if you want to avoid sameness.

In elementary school, I remember sneaking in a pack of strawberry candies one day. Just as I slyly stuck my hand into my backpack to extract a secret treat, Ms. Thomas looked up. I was caught, red-handed. She took the candies from me and said I'd need to wait until after school to get them back.

"But that's not fair!" I said.

"If I let you get candy, then I'd have to let everyone get candy. Either we all get it, or no one gets it. *That's* fair."

Ms. Thomas didn't have the time or the inclination to deal with allowing exceptions. And if you're an elementary school teacher, I get it. But if you deal with grown-ups and want to avoid the downsides of sameness—things like lower productivity, reduced customer satisfaction, and shrinking revenue—you'll need to do exactly what Ms. Thomas said she couldn't do. You'll need to treat people differently.

5. Play a Bigger Game

Leaders waste massive amounts of emotional energy settling the score. Sometimes the waste is obvious, like the decision to subtly sabotage someone else's contributions in a meeting because you think they are getting undue credit. But sometimes spite is hard to spot, like the unconscious decision to make your employees learn things the hard way without support, because you had it tough yourself. Wouldn't it be better for everyone if you just gave the support you wish you had been given?

Is there a cure for spite? If you keep score at work, you won't likely stop. Especially for those of us who are achievement oriented, we crave scoreboards to know how we're doing. Fine, we can keep a scoreboard. But let's choose our scoreboard carefully. Are you playing in a small game against your colleagues or a bigger game against your competition?

Watching a bigger scoreboard often means shifting from a business-unit, functional-area, or single-country perspective to an enterprise-wide, global view. In his book *Collaboration*, Morten Hansen calls this approach "T-Shaped Management."[11] It's T-shaped because there's vertical expertise — within function or geography. And on top of that vertical expertise there's a horizontal bar — the connections across the organization. Hansen argues that modern managers need both the vertical expertise and the horizontal connections. In my words, they need to watch a bigger scoreboard.

I don't think it does much good to tell people to stop keeping score. If you keep score, you're probably not going to stop. A competitive drive is either a deep part of your character, or it's not. If it is, then it's not going away even though that competitive drive has unhealthy, unintended consequences. For example, the marketing manager of the Japanese subsidiary of a company fights for more resources, competing with the marketing manager responsible for the emerging markets in Asia, such as Thailand and Vietnam. The Japanese marketing manager points out the huge revenue streams from big current customers and the threats from serious new competitors. And the emerging markets manager fights back, claiming that a dollar investment in high-growth markets has a much higher return than a dollar invested in slow-growth Japan. So two of the company's most valuable managers fight it out, pouring huge amounts of emotional and intellectual energy into making the case that their region deserves more funding. The scoreboard they are watching is region versus region.

Instead, they should compete against their actual competitors—other global companies with a presence in Japan and in the emerging markets of Southeast Asia. With a T-shaped approach, they would work to out-partner their competition. The challenge is, the degree of partnership isn't as readily measurable as the amount of funding each region gets. So the bigger scoreboard is a bit fuzzy and uncertain. And yet leaders must get comfortable with embracing this fuzziness and resist falling into the trap of competing with colleagues. But don't worry, if you're deeply competitive then focus on beating the hell out of your competitors. Just don't beat the hell out of your friends.

6. Check Up on Others

As we've seen, sometimes we hurt people even when we aim to help them. Our heart's in the right place, but we get into trouble by assuming others want what we want. But sometimes, the story isn't so sunny. Sometimes our heart is in the wrong place. "The Pleasure of Being Nasty" is one of the most interestingly named academic articles I've ever come across. In the article, Klaus Abbink and Abdolkarim Sadrieh examined the research on fairness and found something missing.[12] As I pointed out at the start of this chapter, games like those designed by Ernst Fehr suggest that we don't simply worry about ourselves, we worry about others. And we worry about a general state of justice. We want others to be OK, and we want the world to be OK.

But sometimes, some of us worry about others for a very different reason: because we want them to suffer. As Abbink and Sadrieh say, "There is a danger of overstating the kindness of human nature." I had hoped to reveal in this chapter that all the emerging science on the nature of fairness proves we're more interested in being more altruistic than one might assume. I hadn't planned on showing that sometimes some people are, in fact, out to get us. Thanks for raining on my parade, Abbink and Sadrieh.

Think of their research as a third step in the evolution of economic research on human interaction. First, economists believed that we are all rational actors, looking to improve our own situation. Second, a new set of researchers (Fehr and Rabin) argue that we aren't so selfish after all. Good news: we care about our fellow man. We engage in prosocial behavior. Then Abbink and Sadrieh come along and say, in essence: *Yes, we agree that the old guys got it wrong—we're not simply rational actors trying to make ourselves better. But the new guys—the behavioral economists—get it only half right. We're not only interested in helping our fellow man. Sometimes we want to hurt him, just for the fun of it.*

To test the degree of antisocial behavior, Abbink and Sadrieh invented a game called "The Joy of Destruction." In the game, played at the University of Amsterdam, participants are paid to give their opinions on a series of Dutch advertisements. Two participants who don't know each other work side by side, earning €1.20 for each ad they review. The participants—let's call them Hansel and Gretel—are led to believe they're serving as test customers for ads. Then, after they've given their opinions, but before they are paid the fee, there's an unexpected twist.

Abbink takes one of the participants aside—let's say Hansel—for a private conversation and offers him a surprise opportunity. Hansel can cut Gretel's pay. Gretel will never know it was Hansel who cut the reward; Gretel will be given a bogus explanation related to departmental budget. Hansel won't get any additional pay no matter what he chooses to do. Abbink and Sadrieh designed the game so that the reduction in pay would be completely anonymous and completely without benefit to the punisher. In other words: half of the research subjects in the game have a chance to reduce someone else's pay for no good reason.

The results stun me. Many of the players—up to 40 percent of them—exercised their power to reduce the pay of their new colleague, just for the fun of it, with no benefit to themselves. This is different from the spite in the Clara story. Clara wanted to even things out by punishing her sister. But in this test, some research subjects wanted to hurt others, no matter what the score. Your belief in fairness may lead you to wrongly assume that if you have someone else's best interests at heart, then they also have your best interests at heart.

Some people are, in fact, out to get you. Just for fun. And if you treat them fairly, it can backfire. In the previous side effects, an attempt at fairness backfires because you unintentionally end up hurting someone else. But in the case of antisocial behavior, fairness backfires because you treat someone else fairly, but they intentionally hurt you.

Can you picture someone at work who repeatedly takes advantage of your empathy? Based on an objective assessment of their actions in the past, are you pretty certain this person would cut your pay just for fun? If so, you may be a sucker. It's time to stop.

In follow-up research with two other colleagues, Abbink did new tests that show competition over scarce resources tends to bring out the nastiness.[13] Importantly, they distinguish selfishness from nastiness. The nasty behavior they tested for was about hurting others without helping the subject. So this is different from competitors in a zero-sum game grabbing as much as they can for themselves, even if it hurts others. This is a more subtle link. Abbink and his colleagues showed that simply participating in a more competitive environment caused research subjects to hurt others even *without* helping themselves. This helps to explain why the Dutch students evaluating ads for pay might have been willing to reduce their fellow test subjects' pay. Merely setting up two people working beside each other on the same task felt like a competition to many of the participants. And competitive drive has unintended consequences.

So what's the cure? First, let me say what the cure isn't: it's not paranoia and insularity. The answer is not to assume that everyone is nasty and avoid as many people as possible. And it's a copout for us to assume that our difficult boss or client just takes pleasure from treating us poorly. Once we take that leap, it's tough to listen, learn, and make important self-improvements.

Instead, check others for nastiness. The good news is people tend to be predictable in this regard. In their article "What Do We Expect From

Our Friends?" published in 2010, Stephen Leider[14] and his colleagues built on Abbink's research. They show that our natural state of niceness is pretty constant over time and pretty constant regardless of who we're dealing with. They show that *strangers* who have higher baseline altruism are nicer to each other than *friends* with lower baseline altruism. So it really doesn't matter how well you know someone— it just matters how nice they are. Nice guys are almost always nice, and meanies almost never are.

So the best way to predict if you're dealing with a jerk is to learn about his past behavior. Do you see dead careers and bitter coworkers scattered around his previous projects? If so, stay away. If you suspect your boss has it out for you, check to see if her other employees in other places have thrived. If so, then it's not likely she's suddenly turned evil. When it comes to niceness and meanness, people don't tend to change much. And as a leader, work to decrease the extent that people feel they're competing over a scarce resource, such as a budget, an office, or even your own attention. The more you create an environment of cooperation, the less you can expect the antisocial behavior that punishes the most trusting of your people.

7. Check Up on Yourself

After a successful twenty-year career selling medical devices, Don faced a sudden change. His company was bought, and he was given two options: accept a severance package and leave the company or move to a more junior position on a new team. With two kids in college, Don figured the right answer was the second option. So he swallowed his pride and stepped into the new role with the best of intentions. But little things started to happen that revealed to Don how unfairly he was being treated. His coworkers were much less experienced than he, yet they were given better access to the senior executives who would come in to help close deals. While Don worked to break into new relationships, the other members of his team were given existing accounts with satisfied customers.

After a year, Don's young boss gave him a poor performance review and suggested he could learn a few things from his younger colleagues.

His colleagues got bigger year-end bonuses, which they celebrated on exotic trips. The unfairness mounted until finally Don slipped. He took marketing promotion funds meant for sales events and used them instead to send a sales prospect on a trip. The sales prospect was happy to get the trip and did business with Don. Don preached the value of good ethics to his children, and he'd always taken the high road at work. Misusing marketing funds was exactly the sort of poor choice that Don had lectured others about in the past. But Don was a man of action who couldn't bear to sit quietly and suffer through the unfairness. Instead, he slid down a slippery slope of unethical decisions.

Don's not alone. From executives to politicians to sports heroes, we see examples of slipping all around us. In an attempt to make sense of Barry Bonds's alleged use of steroids, *New York Times* science reporter Benedict Carey explained how cheating can spring from fairness:

> It's often an obsession with fairness that leads people to begin cutting corners in the first place. "Cheating is especially easy to justify when you frame situations to cast yourself as a victim of some kind of unfairness," said Dr. Anjan Chatterjee, a neurologist at the University of Pennsylvania who has studied the use of prescription drugs to improve intellectual performance. "Then it becomes a matter of evening the score; you're not cheating, you're restoring fairness."[15]

If you feel treated unfairly at work, you may begin to rationalize unethical decisions.

We build stories in our brains to make our actions seem in concert with our values. Smart people are really good at this sort of rationalization—they have a really smart lawyer, even if they have a foolish voice in their head for a client. If you've got an above-average IQ, you have an above-average ability to convince yourself that the choices you make are perfectly reasonable. And if you're super smart, you can rationalize some super crazy behavior. Simple messages like: "be ethical" or "do the right thing" won't work, because you'll be able to argue your way into justifying the ethics of your decision.

Do you rationalize your actions as being OK because of how unfairly you were treated? Do you find yourself justifying a decision you made at work to a loved one, even when that loved one never asked you to justify anything? If a voice in your head tells you it's OK to bend the rules because you're just making things even, ignore that voice — it's working against your best long-term interests.

Instead, picture yourself with an angel on one shoulder and the devil on the other. The devil passionately and brilliantly justifies tiny acts of cheating in the name of fairness. The reward network in your brain may want the devil to win the debate, but you need to use the executive functions of your prefrontal cortex to listen hard for the angel on the other shoulder. What's the right thing for you, for the long term? What's the story you want to tell your children, to help them make the right choices? Be the hero of that story now, and resist the urge to use fairness as an excuse to cheat.

Conclusion

Leaders who bully and take advantage of the weak should be found out, labeled, and punished for their unfairness. But in my experience, there aren't too many of these bad guys in the workplace. And I don't think many of those bullies read leadership books in an effort to grow and develop. The more common problem — the one I'm driven to help you solve — is the leader with a heart of gold who unknowingly trips up on her own best intentions.

Many important social changes have come from courageous leaders like Gandhi or King working to create a fairer world. But in both of those cases, these men didn't seek to bring others down; they sought to lift a group up to a just level of opportunity. If we are slighted in the workplace, we're wiser to focus on improving our own situation than on harming others. But here's the trick: our own human nature pulls us toward retribution and spite. It's an unnatural act of courage and discipline to let things go and work on our own progress instead of punishing others.

Putting It into Practice
WHAT IS PROCESS FAIRNESS?

A fair process at work is a just system of allocating rewards and punishments, and an equal opportunity for inputs. The key to honoring fairness as a value in the world of work is to remember that fairness is not equal to sameness.

SO WHAT?

Caring, thoughtful leaders can fall prey to the sacred cow of fairness when they focus on outcomes. When leaders work to ensure a fair outcome at work they turn diverse perspectives into monolithic sameness, increase spiteful score-keeping behavior, reduce the differentiation and meaningfulness of rewards and recognition, and enable ethically questionable decisions. Instead, leaders must train their brains to focus on creating and leading a fair process.

NOW WHAT?

1. **Projection Detection.** It's natural human behavior to project your needs and wants onto others. And, having projected your needs, your sense of fairness leads you to try to meet those projected needs. Resist this trap by raising your self-awareness and question yourself whenever you identify with the needs of another.

2. **Break the Golden Rule.** Just because you want to be treated a certain way doesn't mean that someone else does. Customize your motivation strategy and ensure you're not simply projecting your wants onto other people.

3. **Vive la Différence!** View the world of work with a bias for perceiving differences. Instead of working to identify commonalities, look for — and celebrate — the differences among the people who work for you and with you.

4. **Discriminate Courageously.** To reward those who deserve it, make appropriate exceptions, and dole out penalties when needed, you must possess the courage to recognize and speak difficult truths.

5. **Watch a Bigger Scoreboard.** Don't waste energy worrying if others are getting more than you. Stay competitive, but focus your emotional energy on beating the competition.

6. **Check Up on Others.** If you suspect someone is taking advantage of your fair treatment, check for past behavior to ensure you're not working with a meanie.

7. **Check Up on Yourself.** Watch out for the temptation to rationalize unethical decisions when you feel you've been treated unfairly.

7

Obsessive Harmonious Passion

I learned firsthand how passion can backfire in my first year of business school. Most students work in big companies, banks, or consulting firms before starting Duke's MBA program. I, on the other hand, had worked at a small liberal arts college in South Carolina. My undergraduate degree was in English, while most of my peers had business, economics, or engineering degrees. But there was one thing we all had in common: we were competing for jobs. I had risked my family's financial health by going into significant debt to fund the MBA. With two young kids, finding a job that paid well enough to pay back my student loans was critical. For me, the job search was important for functional and emotional reasons. I needed a good job to repay debt, and I needed many job offers to prove to myself that I belonged in business school. I dedicated myself to the goal of getting as many job offers as possible and decided that no one would outwork me.

The job search process starts even before classes do. Within the first few weeks I had tried and failed to get on the interview list at each of the elite investment banks and consulting firms. My attempts to frame my background as relevant for those industries had failed. I didn't want to be a banker or consultant, but that wasn't relevant to my objective. The only thing that I watched was the scoreboard that showed how many offers I had for summer internships — the gateway to one of the high-paying jobs I sought. While my new corporate friends started to accumulate offers, my score remained at zero.

Over the winter holidays the school's marketing club sponsored a trip to New York City for interested students to interview for summer internships in the marketing departments of big corporations. Companies from New York, New Jersey, and Connecticut had agreed to meet with Duke MBA students who wanted to work in marketing. Finally, this was my shot. Many of my peers with undergraduate degrees from Ivy League schools already had offers for summer internships by this point, so the field wasn't as crowded with all-stars. And the "quant jocks" with brilliant mathematical skills weren't interested in the more moderately paying marketing jobs. Although I wasn't passionate about the idea of working in corporate marketing, I was very passionate about getting job offers. By now, masking my insecurity that I didn't measure up was an even bigger motivator than feeding my kids. They had grandparents who wouldn't let them starve, but there was no backup plan for my fragile ego.

During the week, as a way to save money, I shared a cheap hotel room with another guy interviewing for marketing jobs in the New York area. As the week went on, I made the case that I had the perfect mix of experience and interest to market exactly what that company happened to be selling, whether it was medicine, soft drinks, credit cards, or clothes. And each day ended the same way: my roommate for the week made it to a second-round interview while I was told that I wasn't a fit. Of course, now I agree completely with the wisdom of the managers who interviewed me, and I'm grateful that they weeded me out as a bad fit. But at the time, I didn't feel grateful. I just felt defeated. These rejections had proved my deepest insecurities and anxieties — I didn't measure up. On the last night, after my defeat was complete, I sat silently in my bed, fuming, trying to find some distraction in David Letterman's top-ten list. I went into the bathroom during an ad and came back out and found my roommate-for-the-week watching Jay Leno. Normally my preference for Letterman over Leno is slight, but on that night it felt enormous. I had been losing all week, but I was going to win this one. After attempting to use rational arguments, I reached for the remote to change it myself. He reached for it at the same time, and we knocked over a lamp in the process. As the bulb fluttered and then fizzled out on top of the cracked ceramic base of the lamp, I muttered a few words. That broken lamp finally made the truth bright enough for me to see it even through the dense fog of my desperate drive for a job.

I laid back down on my twin mattress and glared at the water-stained ceiling. With the cackles of Jay Leno in the background I came to the realization that my plan was failing. I always figured if I wanted something badly enough I could fight through and get it. Passion mattered most. Didn't it?

Good Passion, Bad Passion

Passion can make someone who is good at their job even better. Passion gives leaders fuel to keep fighting through disappointment and make great things happen. A passionate leader inspires others to care more and give their best. Add passion and the normal tasks of day-to-day work can turn into accomplishments of significance. Passionate people roll out of bed with fire in their belly and their eyes on the prize. The leader who manages a team of passionate people can spend less time trying to motivate them and more time getting things done.

But passion has a dark side. It can lead to burnout that lowers performance. Some people ruminate about the things they care about so much that they can't concentrate on or enjoy other parts of their lives. Passion for one thing can crowd out other things, including even your values. And, as you'll soon see from research, passion can lead to sickness and physical injury.

Passion can be good or bad because it can come from different places. The source of the passion determines whether it's good or bad. Robert Vallerand, professor of psychology at the University of Quebec, has done more than anyone to understand this distinction. Vallerand created the dualistic model of passion, which contrasts healthy, harmonious passion with unhealthy, obsessive passion. While his theory is informed by a wide-sweeping review of the nature of this much-studied element of human nature going back to classical philosophers Plato and Aristotle, I find his modern, experimental research uncovering the source of passion to be most fascinating. Vallerand and others who have continued his research stream have conducted hundreds of studies to demonstrate precisely how destructive the obsessive type can be and where it comes from. According to Vallerand, "People with a predominant obsessive passion have a contingent sense of self-worth and life satisfaction."[1] So if your passion is obsessive, it affects your own self-esteem, which affects everything else you do.

My problem in business school was that I needed traditional job offers to help me feel that I was worthy and belonged to the group. I didn't want any of the jobs I interviewed for. What I wanted was to help leaders learn, but I thought that was a foolish ambition that would have to wait until later. Luckily I discovered Duke CE and had the pleasure of working on what I wanted to work on. In fact, I worked nearly full-time at Duke CE during the second year of my MBA program. I loved the work, and it made me a better father and a better student. I had finally stumbled onto harmonious passion.

At the time, Vallerand had just begun his research and I had never heard of him. But I had certainly heard of passion. My family encouraged me to find my passion. Graduation speeches urged me to follow my passion. Experts everywhere celebrate the virtue of passion. So when I felt passion for the job search, I assumed it was a good thing.

People who are passionate about birdwatching describe themselves as *birders*. People who are passionate about working at IBM call themselves *IBMers*. Identity doesn't make passion obsessive. It's the process by which a passion becomes internalized that marks the difference. In Vallerand's somewhat technical language, the difference is "autonomous internalization" versus "controlled internalization." If a birder decides of her own accord that she loves the intellectual, competitive, and artistic mix of scouring the planet to find birds, then her passion for birding is likely autonomously internalized and, therefore, healthy and harmonious. On the other hand, if a birder feels driven to prove herself to her skeptical father by becoming the first American to spot the Kakapo, a flightless parrot in New Zealand, she probably has the unhealthy, obsessive passion that comes from controlled internalization. People with harmonious passion engage in an activity because they want to. People with obsessive passion engage in an activity because they feel they must.

Blanka Rip, a young French-Canadian psychology professor at Carnegie Mellon, studied under Vallerand. While other scholars had shown that obsessive passion can hurt people by making them less satisfied with their lives, Rip wanted to know just how badly obsessive passion hurts. Can it, for example, cause physical pain? She put obsessive passion to the test in a world in which the dark side of passion can become physically apparent: professional dance. Dancers experience a wide range of injuries, and not mere blisters on their toes. Crippling injuries to the lower back, neck, ankles, and feet savage the careers of many dancers, making an outwardly beautiful art quietly painful. Rip sought to understand the link between dancers' motivation to dance and the injuries they suffer.

Rip analyzed injury rates in two different groups of dancers. Some of them felt that dance was the only thing that turned them on and agreed they were often unable to stop thinking about dance. Based on Vallerand's research, she classified those dancers as being obsessively passionate. Meanwhile, Rip considered a dancer to be motivated by harmonious passion when they agreed with statements like "dance reflects the qualities I like about myself" and "dance is in harmony with my other life activities." The two groups of dancers weren't different in ability in performance or achievement. They were all volunteers of similar skill and experience from the Department of Dance at the University of Quebec. The question that Rip's experiment would answer was: would the dancers motivated by an obsessive passion have more injuries than the dancers who loved to dance but loved other things as well?

As it turns out, obsessive passion is very bad for a dancer's health. There was no meaningful relationship between having harmonious passion and having chronic injuries. It would be wrong to conclude from the study that harmony prevents injury. But the correlation between obsessive passion and chronic injuries was significant and positive. Though there's no guarantee that obsession will lead to injury, it does seem that it's not so healthy for dancers to be exclusively committed to dance.[2]

How does obsessive passion lead to injury? Obsessive dancers are less likely to take time off after an injury and less likely to seek the help of a professional. The obsessive dancers also reported that they were much more likely to report that they considered their personal pride when deciding to seek help for an injury. For harmoniously passionate dancers, the choice to seek help for an injury was a simple one based on the presence of pain. But for the obsessed, the decision to ask for help was much more complex.

The Sustaining Strength of Harmonious Passion

In a master class at the Longy School of Music in Cambridge, Massachusetts, cellist Yo-Yo Ma taught local kids about playing cello and managing energy. As reported in a 2000 *Harvard Magazine* article, one girl, Lauren, was exhausted after playing just the prelude to a concerto. Ma coached her on managing energy, pointing out the physical demands of playing the instrument. "Go with the energy around you . . . use the power of the orchestra to help you, that's the secret." Ma is more than a master teacher and cellist—he's a world class manager of energy.[3]

Scott Barry Kaufman, the cognitive scientist at NYU who described the neurochemical payoff of novelty in Chapter Four, has also studied the way the brain behaves in passionate people. He points to Ma as the quintessential example of harmonious passion.[4] Ma started studying cello when he was four and took lessons from a Juilliard professor while in high school. But he turned down the opportunity to go to college for music performance, deciding instead to get a broader liberal arts education. More obsessive musicians would have felt a compulsion to put performance above everything, but Ma sought a broader approach.

In the *Harvard Magazine* article Ma credits his time as an under-graduate for broadening his horizons. Later he became known as one of classical music's great crossover artists. But he's been crossing over for most of his life. "Harvard was the first place in my life where I was systematically introduced to different worlds and ways of thinking. I learned there how science and art are joined under philosophy." Ma continues to stretch, playing with a wide range of collaborators from jazz to bluegrass to gospel. And Ma has experimented with multime-dia, having ice dancers and Kabuki performers accompany his playing of Bach suites. Sometimes he stretches so far that he irks those who defend the status quo. Leon Kirchner, one of Ma's music professors at Harvard, called Ma's experiments with multimedia "baloney." But Ma doesn't feel the obsessive need to excel in one direction only. He feels free to explore.

Harmony isn't found only at Harvard. You can find it on a tennis court or in a nail salon. Serena Williams, one of the greatest tennis play-ers in the history of the world, is a certified nail technician. Why?

"No one likes getting their nails done more than I do," Williams posted on her GlobalGrind blog. "As a matter of fact I go every four days to get a manicure and every seven days for a pedicure. So, I had a bril-liant idea to get certified to be a nail tech."[5] Williams has also released a line of designer clothes, handbags, and jewelry. Some view her var-ied interests as harmful distractions that reveal a lack of respect for the game. As Peter Bodo, senior editor of *Tennis Magazine*, sees it: "Serena's problem appears to be that she likes the reward (celebrity and money) but not the process. She would like to win the Australian title and any number of other tournaments, but she hates having to go through the motions — you know, the long practice sessions, the diet, the gym work-outs and even that messy business of playing matches."[6]

That would be a very fair critique of my dedication to running cross country in high school. But Williams is one of the most accomplished women's tennis players in history. By some measures, she's the *most* accomplished. As of July 2012, she ranked #1 on the list of women's career prize-money leaders with $38 million. And it's not close — her sister Venus was second with $28 million and Kim Clijsters was third with $24 million. Yet Bodo and many other tennis commentators insist Williams could do so much more if she only put her mind to it. Williams has found sustaining success through a harmonious passion that looks like slacking off to those used to seeing only obsession. The word passion is derived from the Latin word *pati*, meaning "to suffer, endure." How can an athlete be passionate if she doesn't suffer?

Serena Williams won the gold medal in the 2012 London Olympics while playing "the most dominant stretch of tennis in her illustrious career," according to *Yahoo! Sports* tennis writer Chris Chase.[7] Her gold in London came two months before her thirty-first birthday. One month later, she won the U.S. Open. While Andy Roddick was being celebrated for his final appearance at the end of his career, Williams, who is one year older than Roddick, was still playing her best tennis. Perhaps the harmony of her life — tennis balanced with fashion — added years to her career that a more obsessive athlete would have missed. And there's certainly nothing bland about Williams's approach to balance — she finds harmonious passion through embracing wildly different aspects of her personality.

In a world that expects an obsessive passion to crowd out all other aspects of a person's life, harmonious passion stands out. It's easy to mistake for being laid-back or "type B." So, Serena Williams should stop fooling around with fashion, and Yo-Yo Ma should stick to classical music and stop experimenting across genres. When I describe the notion of harmonious versus obsessive passion to leaders, I typically hear back from them something like: "I get it. If you're willing to accept a little less success, you can have a much happier life overall."

But that's not the point. Harmonious passion isn't about lowering standards or wimping out. Rather, it's world-class leadership that comes from a healthier, more resilient, more sustainable source.

The studies that Vallerand and his colleagues have done show that people don't sacrifice performance in order to gain harmony. Instead, it's harmonious passion that offers something extra. Harmonious passion in one activity leads to high performance in the activity and overall happiness with other aspects of life. The lawyer who enjoys gardening and follows her passion to personalize her lawn finds herself generally happier, and that general happiness spills over into work. Meanwhile the lawyer who feels compelled to win the best lawn contest that begins in her mind every time she drives into her neighborhood is less likely to find peace at home, and that dissatisfaction makes everything in her life just a little bit worse.

Harmonious passion in an activity at work or play corresponds to a happier life. But being engaged in obsessive passion in any activity correlates to an overall sense of unhappiness with life. Of course there's no way to say that one thing leads to another. Scientists often can't prove with certainty that one thing leads to another. But it's safe to say that obsessive passion isn't usually a part of a happy leader's life. Let's focus, then, on how to make sure your passion is harmonious.

Seven Steps to Make Your Passion More Harmonious

Passion is an important ingredient in the recipe for leadership success. But to make sure your passion is harmonious, you should take a hard look at the source of that passion. Are you fueled by hope and happiness as you run toward a goal? Or are you running away from fear and insecurities? Get to know the source of your passion, find a support system to keep you healthy and out of trouble, and look beyond your own interests to enjoy the sustaining power of harmonious passion.

1. Find Your Shard of Glass

The first step to finding more harmonious passion is to find less obsessive passion. Because obsessive passions crowd out harmonious ones, you'll need to recognize and remove your workplace obsessions. In order to do that, you'll need to identify the source. A chip on your shoulder can motivate you to run through a wall, but running through walls hurts. Take a deep breath and a hard look at that chip. And if you need to get through a wall, find a ladder. To help you identify and eliminate the obsessive chip on your shoulder, let's go to the movies.

I lead a workshop called "The Story of You." In this program I help participants develop their own personal leadership story, based on a three-act structure learned from Hollywood screenwriters. I'm fascinated by the link between character development on screen and character development in the leaders who run big organizations. I started to wonder about this connection when the same film clips kept showing up in every leadership development program. For example, *Braveheart* teaches how to energize a group, *As Good as It Gets* reveals the painful process of developing emotional intelligence, and *Invictus* demonstrates how a connection to a larger purpose can motivate a team.

If there were insights worthy of a leader's attention in those movies, there must be a screenwriter behind the words who had that insight. I read several screenwriting books and attended a few seminars for screenwriters to learn more about the craft. One of the most interesting and helpful perspectives I found was in *Save the Cat*, Blake Snyder's book on screenwriting. In Chapter Four on creativity I describe Snyder's approach as an example of the form that screenwriters can use to give their ideas structure.

The book's methodical deconstruction of the fifteen beats of Hollywood screenplays seemed like a solution to a puzzle that I didn't know existed. Snyder passed away in 2009, at the age of fifty-one. He left behind a rich legacy that's helped many successful screenwriters. One point that's relevant for leaders to help them find the source of their potentially obsessive passion is the "shard of glass" that a hero examines about 75 percent of the way through a movie. As Snyder described in a blog posting shortly before his untimely death, "The hero is forced to face an ugly truth about himself that he's been resisting . . . That's the 'shard of glass,' that sharp-edged incident, bad behavior, tough truth or wrong done and absorbed that the hero swallowed a long time ago. Skin has grown up around its hard corners, but it's in there — deep — and it must be pulled out and looked at and dealt with."[8]

Good films resonate when they teach us something that feels immediately true even though we haven't considered it before. Just as fictional heroes have a shard of glass, many leaders have an issue that needs to be "pulled out and looked at and dealt with." That issue, buried deep, can often be the source of obsessive passion.

Three questions can help a leader find their shard: What do you need to prove? To whom? And why? Find the answers to those questions, reflect on the activities you're most passionate about, and you may find an interesting connection.

Just as a hero in a film can have a dramatic moment when she finally confronts a weakness she's buried, a leader can gain real credibility by coming clean to her team and admitting that she's been trying too hard to prove something that's been driving an unhealthy passion for herself and her team. People don't expect leaders to be perfect, but they do hope that they'll be honest and brave.

2. Lead from Behind

The thirty workers at the small ad agency squeezed into the conference room for the weekly Monday morning meeting. Although the meeting looked like work, it felt like church, with the agency's CEO, Mike Armstrong (name changed to protect the passionate) serving as pastor. Like a Sunday church service, every week at the Armstrong Agency started with the same ritual. The boss welcomed his team with a beaming smile, reviewed some quick logistics, and then he brought the passion. Each time, Armstrong implored the staff to rise up to that week's biggest challenge. Even if the challenge involved the normal tasks of installing a new version of Photoshop, going to a lithographer for a press run, or meeting with the local television station to discuss the upcoming season of programming. Armstrong was fired up about life, and he believed that was the only way to live. An important part of his identity was the role of "cheerleader in chief." He waved his arms, clapped his hands, and spoke with urgency until his voice hoarsened. And sometimes, when Armstrong remarked on how special each person in the room was to him, his eyes glistened and he choked back tears. After this burst of emotion, the staff would clap in support. And then they would return to their desks, check their e-mail, and start the day.[9]

Passion like this can be exhausting. Sometimes the leaders burn out, but that's not what happened in Armstrong's case. Propelled by a rare mix of determination and grit, Armstrong just kept going. But his staff wasn't as resilient. Although they were entranced by his energy at first, they grew exhausted after a few months. Some people checked out mentally, viewing the mandatory meetings as a distraction to make it through, while others checked out literally and found a new job. The turnover at the company was incredibly high, with the average employee tenure being about eighteen months. Armstrong had a way of rationalizing the turnover — if people left it was because they didn't "get it." But he spent a lot of time and money recruiting and training new people in hopes of finding new followers.

Perhaps you were attracted to leadership because you wanted to stand and deliver inspiration to a room full of people. That may be your need. But true leaders put the needs of their people and their organizations above their own. Before you give that fiery speech to your team, ask if they need it. If you feel the need to motivate some people, maybe you can volunteer to coach a youth sports team. Sometimes leaders are better leading from the back of the room. As Nelson Mandela said, "Put others in front, especially when you celebrate victory when nice things occur. You take the front line when there is danger. Then people will appreciate your leadership."

3. Stop Proving Yourself Right

In only two years, Grace Turner (not her real name) had built a very strong reputation as a CPM (Channel Partner Manager) at a computer hardware company. She got the strongest possible performance reviews and was identified as a high-potential leader. CPMs like Grace lead key relationships with her company's distribution partners. Almost every-thing the company sold went through a partner, so the role was critical to its overall success. Many CPMs viewed the role as being primarily about sales, and they worked hard to persuade their partners to sell more products from their company than from competitors. But Grace took a very different approach. She viewed her role as being an advocate for her partners. She fought hard to give them market information and leads, and never pushed product. Other CPMs would "jam" deals at the end of the quarter by dint of force and enthusiasm, but not Grace. She got to know the leaders at the partner companies. Some of the executives at the companies she partnered with would even bring Grace in to interview potential job candidates. They considered Grace to be a deeply trusted adviser.

After her third successful year as a CPM, Grace was presented with two new opportunities: become a manager of CPMs or take an enterprise sales job. The safe thing would be to move up into managing CPMs. But she felt the sales job was an exciting opportunity for her to get different experience. Like the trick-or-treaters in Chapter Two on balance, she thought she would enjoy variety. And even more than that, she was going to prove a point. Enterprise sales professionals could be successful with the same long-term view she had. She had never faced anything but success in her career, and now her success in sales would show that the sales guys didn't need to be the "bad cop" to the CPMs "good cop," as they often did. So she stepped confidently into her new role as a sales executive.

But Grace struggled. She treated her customers the same way she had treated her partners. Sales professionals from competitors offered time-limited discounts and used pushy sales tactics that Grace refused to employ. Eventually her long-term focus would pay off, she believed. And maybe it would have, but at the end of the year, the team's numbers were down. And Grace's numbers were especially bad. She had several deals near closing, but she wouldn't push the deals because she didn't believe they were in her customer's best long-term interest. Why should her own company's billing cycle influence a customer's IT strategy? When her boss pushed her to close the deals, she refused.

Though her boss couldn't fire her because of her track record of good reviews, he gave her a bad review and eliminated her position. Once that happened she had thirty days to interview internally to find a new job. By that time, her old CPM job had been filled, and her terrible performance review prevented her from finding a new role. When she couldn't find a role, she had no choice but to accept a severance package. In one year she'd gone from being a highly promising, fast-moving young professional to being jobless.

Grace had been courageous and passionate. And she'd also been stubborn. She was going to prove that the enterprise salespeople didn't need to be so pushy at her company. Her attitude and skills made her a perfect fit for the CPM role, but a lousy fit for the sales role at the same company. Perhaps with another year in the role, a more supportive environment, and a better boss, she could have developed into a strong salesperson. But in her company, sales is an unforgiving job function. She knew that before she took the role, but she was determined to teach those cowboys in sales a lesson.

I love Nike's slogan, *Just Do It*. I'm moved by Seth Godin's *Poke the Box*, which is a leadership manifesto in favor of just doing it. But before you do it, ask yourself: Are you motivated to prove someone wrong? Do you have a chip on your shoulder? Maybe that motivation isn't a healthy one that will lead you to happiness. Sometimes leaders need the advice to spring to action and jump for opportunities.

But sometimes they need the wisdom and restraint to decline an adventure. The key is to avoid the opportunities you seek out simply to prove something to yourself or anyone else. Don't pursue a new job because you want to teach the group a lesson. When you do take on a new role, be a learner, not a teacher.

4. Start Proving Yourself Wrong

Dorothy Martin thought the world was going to end at midnight on December 20, 1954, as a result of a massive flood. She didn't reach out to the press to announce this event or advertise widely for followers. She didn't argue with anyone who disagreed with her about her prediction. Getting swept away in a flood would be their loss, not hers. A group of about fifteen people agreed with Dorothy, and they were all relieved to learn that a flying saucer would be taking them to the planet Clarion just before the flood. They gathered at Dorothy's home to wait for their rescue. But the flying saucer didn't come, and neither did the flood. Do you think Dorothy changed her apocalyptic belief in the face of this sequence of events? Or do you think she kept the same steadfast belief and just found a new date on which the world would end?

She did neither. Instead, she immediately switched from being a quiet believer to becoming a loud evangelist. By around 4 AM on December 21, she said she had received a message from Clarion that the apocalypse would be delayed. And then she did something she had never done before. She called a newspaper reporter to spread the news.

We know about this switch because Leon Festinger, a social psychologist from the University of Minnesota, was one of the people with Dorothy. Personally, I discovered the story in Robert Cialdini's excellent book *Influence: The Psychology of Persuasion*. Festinger and some of his students had embedded themselves in the cult as a way to try to understand more about the way people with strongly held beliefs respond to disconfirming evidence. He was just beginning to test out cognitive dissonance, an idea he'd formed to express how hard our brains will work to avoid the uncomfortable tension of learning we were wrong all along. As Festinger wrote in his book *When Prophecy Fails* about the cult members, "only hours earlier they had shunned newspaper reporters and felt that the attention they were getting in the press was painful, yet now they became avid seekers of publicity."[10]

Festinger explained that Dorothy needed others to believe her because her belief was now threatened. In Festinger's words, when people are confronted with evidence that disputes a core belief, they "may show a new fervor about convincing and converting other people to their view."[11]

The point of Festinger's story isn't that Dorothy was a wacko. While her beliefs were quite abnormal, Festinger showed that the way she dealt with her beliefs was perfectly normal. When presented with evidence that our most treasured beliefs are wrong, our first instinct is to double down. There's a war going on in our brains between memory and discovery. With disciplined mindfulness, leaders can win this war. But too often a leader becomes a passionate advocate for a belief precisely at the moment he is presented with evidence that contradicts that belief.

Leaders can fight through mountains of disconfirming evidence to prove themselves right. And the more passionate they are, the more zealously they'll fight.

Consider a brand manager at Big Global Tech Company (BGTC) who believes the brand is in trouble if they don't centralize all activities at his large, global enterprise. "We can't let people in Hong Kong hear a different message about our product than people in Paris." So everyone begins to move in lockstep, saying the same messages about the product. And sales drop. But instead of accepting that feedback, the brand manager advocates with more strength than ever why the company needs to globalize more. The world is complex, so the brand manager won't have any shortage of data to make his point. Maybe the problem was in local language translation or poor timing. Maybe we need to give the market time to get used to the new approach. To avoid any doubt creeping into his brain, the brand manager needs more people than ever to believe that globalization is the right approach.

Or consider the head of a business unit at a large aerospace company who believes his firm should buy a young, growing competitor. The executive at the large company hires an investment bank and law firm to conduct due diligence on the startup, and the data suggests the acquisition is a good idea. But the HR staff at the company warns that the cultures of the two companies are so wildly different that the pace of integration will be slowed. The leader running the business unit tells himself that the HR group just doesn't want to deal with the extra work the acquisition will create, and maybe they're afraid of losing their jobs as part of eliminating redundancies. So after the merger goes through and the culture clash leads to poor performance, the leader can simply blame his HR staff for not working hard enough to make the transition smooth. And perversely, it's at this point, as the wisdom of the acquisition looks most in question, that Festinger predicts the executive will start looking hard for the next acquisition. At a deep level, he needs to prove he was right.

The best defense against brainwashing is deprogramming. Can you think of anytime recently when you ratcheted up your advocacy in favor of a point of view even in the face of some evidence against your side?

Write down (writing helps you make it real) every piece of data you can think of to prove yourself wrong.

I don't know if you're right or wrong. But I do know we humans have the tendency to dig our heels in and passionately defend our perspective exactly when that perspective has been proved to be vulnerable.

5. Stay Healthy with the Buddy System

Remember Blanka Rip's study on dance? The more obsessive a dancer's passion, the less likely they were to seek out medical help for an injury. The issue of injury and obsession is not limited to dancers. In January 2006, the day before he was to fly from Tokyo to Detroit for the North American International Auto Show, one of Toyota's top engineers died due to restricted blood flow to his heart. The man's name wasn't revealed when the Japanese Health Ministry ruled that he suffered *karoshi*, which is literally translated as death from overwork. According to the *New York Times*, he "regularly worked nights and weekends" and "was grappling with shipping a model to the pivotal trade show." He had been "under severe pressure as the lead engineer in developing a hybrid version for Toyota's blockbuster Camry line."[12] It's impossible to know for sure if this man's passion for work came from a healthy, autonomous desire to work for the intrinsic rewards it provided him. But I doubt it. Feeling compelled to perform in order to live up to your own standard is a hallmark of unhealthy, obsessive passion.

For the obsessively passionate leader, severe pressure can be especially dangerous. More harmonious leaders have invested in other aspects of their lives that they can draw on in times of crisis. But obsessive passion crowds out everything except the object of the passion. Intense pressure at work traps the obsessive leader. Leaders who feel compelled to be passionate about work don't have an obsession switch to turn off. But they may be able to get someone else to tell them when they need some recovery time.

Leaders should ask a trusted work friend to help them decide if they need to take a break. Just as football players must get the OK from the team doctor before they can return to the game after an injury, leaders need someone else to tell them they need to sit out the next play. A smart friend who knows you well can tell you if your passion is backfiring at work. If your passion is obsessive, it's easy to trick yourself, so find someone who will give you the hard truth. And then trust whatever she says. If you're so focused on achieving a short-term target that you've become deaf to what others need from you, your friend can help you see this.

Consider the times in your job when you find your heart racing because of pressure. Do you have a friendly colleague who can help give you an outside perspective? Ask her if you seem too narrowly focused on the task ahead. Ask her what you might be missing. And offer to do the same for her. But please don't use this advice as an excuse to turn everything you do into a two-person group project. Make sure you limit these check-ins to the occasional moments when there is real danger of being derailed by obsession, and keep the conversations short and focused on the single purpose. Otherwise, you'll fall into the trap of automatic collaboration as you try to avoid obsessive passion.

6. Stay Out of Trouble with the Buddy System

Born in Poland in 1879, Francizck Koystra left home when he was a teenager to train as a cook in some of the finest restaurants in Vienna, Austria. In 1905, Koystra moved to America to pursue his dream of opening and operating an upscale restaurant. He settled in Newark and shortened his name to Frank. Frank married twenty-year-old Helen Frukar, also a Polish immigrant, in 1910, and one year later they had a son, Eddie. Frank tried many times to open a restaurant, but failed to get the funding. His command of the English language was poor, and attempts with the bankers fell through. After a few failed efforts at pursuing his original dream, Frank opened a butcher shop instead.

Frank and Helen were proud to watch Eddie grow up with a strong command of the English language and a keen interest in science. While he lived a comfortable life, eventually running a local tavern in addition to the butcher shop, Frank never realized the ambition that had brought him from Poland to Austria to New Jersey. So Frank deferred his dream down a generation to his son Eddie, hoping that he might rise to be as successful as the many other first-generation Americans in their neighborhood. As a young boy, Eddie thrilled his parents when he revealed that he would grow up to be a doctor.

But like his father, Eddie never achieved his career goal. Instead of becoming a doctor, Eddie worked in a series of on-again, off-again jobs, including as a gym teacher and pharmaceutical salesperson, struggling to make ends meet for his six children. Eddie Koystra raised his family in a three-bedroom house in Jersey City, New Jersey. Eddie was known in his neighborhood as a demanding father and heavy drinker who yelled at his six children and his wife, Martha, so much that the other children in the neighborhood were afraid to visit the Koystra home.

Two generations of Koystras had now failed to live up to their dreams. But the third generation would be different. Determined to see that the family finally live up to their potential and achieve the success that neither he nor his father had, Eddie focused his time and attention on his children. Frank Koystra had claimed to come from a long line of Polish warriors, dating back to the Crusades, and, like his father, Eddie believed the Koystra clan was destined for greatness in America. He insisted that his children set high goals and overcome every obstacle in their path.

The eldest of the six Koystra children, Martha (named for her mother), was a pleaser and achiever who would not let her father down. A straight-A student in high school, she won a partial scholarship to elite Barnard College in New York City. While at Barnard, Martha was a double major in history and architectural history, and she took a part-time job as a model to help pay the tuition bills not covered by her scholarship. As with everything else she did, Martha did not merely participate in modeling—she succeeded. She was featured in several national television and magazine advertisements for brands such as Breck hair spray, Lady Clairol, and Tareyton cigarettes.

Young Martha was a Koystra whose ambition would not be denied. Her passion was fueled by three generations, over eighty years. Every step up the ladder of success seemed like a piece of evidence to make her case that she would be different. After marrying Yale law student

Andy Stewart, Martha — now Martha Stewart — gave birth to a daughter, Alexis, and began a successful career as a stockbroker.

Martha Stewart's focus on achieving success as a student, model, and stockbroker was followed by success as a caterer, author, television personality, and media executive. She had to show to the world — and to herself — that her career trajectory would be different from her father's and grandfather's. Multigenerational drive isn't typically healthy, autonomous, harmonious passion. Instead, this sort of drive often contains the uncontrollable urge to prove something. It's a chip-on-the-shoulder drive to set the record straight on a family's place in the world.

This single-minded passion never let Martha down — until she faced her greatest challenge. In June 2002, the U.S. House Energy and Commerce Committee announced they were investigating Stewart's trade of ImClone stock six months earlier. Stewart, sixty-one at the time, knew exactly what to do: win at all costs. She simply would not let her lifetime of work and sacrifice be destroyed by the allegations that she had made an illegal stock trade.

At first, Stewart's passion seemed to have paid off once again. Judge Miriam Cederbaum threw out the securities fraud charges against Stewart, saying "no jury could feasibly find it to be accurate." But the federal grand jury in Manhattan indicted Stewart on charges of obstruction of justice, conspiracy, and making false statements as part of the initial investigation into insider trading. Found guilty of these charges, Stewart lost her television show, resigned from the board of the company she had founded, and folded her magazine. Stewart served a five-month prison term at Alderson Federal Prison in Alderson, West Virginia, followed by five months of house arrest in which she was forced to wear an ankle bracelet during her few trips outside of her home.

During the investigation into insider trading, and, more to the point, during her entire career, Stewart's will was focused on one goal: winning whatever challenge currently lay before her, at any cost. That determined focus on winning helped her achieve heights that her father and grandfather could never have imagined. But the pressure of finally living up to three generations of promise set in motion a single-minded, obsessive passion that led her to a prison sentence and public disgrace. Either because no one warned her or because she couldn't hear the warnings, Stewart's passion veered out of control.

Leaders need others to help keep them in check. Ask a trusted friend if you are at risk of taking your passion for work too far. And if you are, stop, before it's too late.

7. Look Outside Yourself

People who suffer mild bouts of depression are sometimes advised by a counselor to help themselves by helping others. The idea is to start to get out of your own funk by helping someone else get out of theirs. Plus, it gives you a healthy perspective about your own life. So instead of advising patients to go to a festival and surround themselves with happy people, therapists might advise those with mild, occasional depression to volunteer at a shelter as part of their treatment plan.

Forgetting about your own needs and taking care of others can be good advice for anyone looking for their passion. In one of the *Harvard Business Review*'s most popular blog postings ever, "To Find Happiness, Forget About Your Passion," Oliver Segovia encourages leaders not to look inside themselves to find what they're passionate about.[13] Instead, they should look around the world for big problems that need to be solved. It turns out that looking for motivation outside of yourself is one of the most important ways to ensure your passion is harmonious instead of obsessive. Segovia contrasts two women, one who followed her inner passion to teach and one who worked to help others who needed to learn. The first woman reflected on what made her happiest and decided it was teaching. She quit her job, spent over seven years struggling in academia, and became socially withdrawn. For her, the path of looking inside herself has not led to happiness.

Umaimah Mendhro, on the other hand, continues to be driven by the sustaining passion that can only come from looking outside of yourself. Mendhro grew up in rural Pakistan and then Saudi Arabia, with dreams of making it to the States. Once she did, she started dreaming of going back. As an MBA student at Harvard, Umaimah returned to her home village in Akri, Pakistan. She resolved to build a school there to make sure that other kids might have the same chance to develop intellectually that she had.

Umaimah started a nonprofit company, dreamfly, that built a school in Akri, her birthplace, and also in India, Rwanda, and Afghanistan. And she took a position at Microsoft as a director of an internal start-up group, enabling her to learn entrepreneurial lessons to apply to dreamfly. Instead of a single-minded focus on the nonprofit, she said she "wanted to have that richness in my life of mixing for-profit and social cause. I think there's a lot I can take from one world and apply to another— and I specifically valued the richness, diversity, sometimes inherent conflict, most of the times complementary opportunities, of living in these two worlds simultaneously."[14]

Her focus on others isn't limited to the nonprofit. Inside Microsoft, she has several younger people she mentors, and she makes her work as mentor a top priority. I asked Umaimah if working to help others inside Microsoft or back in her home village was more fulfilling than simply trying to gratify her own needs. She paused. "I just don't think there's any other way. My parents were doctors who took care of sick people in the village. Thinking about others is just the way I live."[15]

Instead of looking inside yourself to find your passion, can you look around you to find someone who could use your help? You're more likely to find healthy passion that way.

Conclusion

Too often, leaders make a tradeoff they don't need to: Do I want to perform at a high level, or do I want to be relaxed and peaceful? You don't need to suffer to be fully committed to your work. You don't need to prove anything to anyone. You don't need to sacrifice health and harmony to get results.

Leaders can become brainwashed by their own passion when they need something so desperately that they shut their brains off and ignore or counterargue any disconfirming evidence. They can cause people to become burned out by their incessant cheerleading, or they can encourage sustaining passion by leading from behind. Leaders can bend their own values because of an obsessive passion, or they can rely on a friend to catch them before they fall. They can look inside and try to find their passion, which often leads to self-obsession. Or they can look out into the world to find a problem that needs to be addressed.

If your passion is harmonious, you can enjoy high performance and high satisfaction. If you've already found that harmonious passion at work, be a leader and help someone else find theirs.

Putting It into Practice
WHAT IS HARMONIOUS PASSION?

Harmonious passion is caring about something at work in a way that improves not only that activity but everything else you do. The part of your job that you are most passionate about should live in harmony with other aspects of your job and your life, making everything better. The key to honoring passion as a value in the world of work is to look to its source: intrinsic passion (the kind that comes from within) is good fuel for success in the long run. Beware passion with its roots in insecurity or a need to prove something.

SO WHAT?

Passion can become obsessive and unhealthy. Obsessive passion stems from a lack of self-esteem or a desire for social belonging. Leaders who need to prove something to themselves or someone else can have high performance in the short term, but eventually obsessive passion crowds out other aspects of a leader's life that sustain the leader, thereby leading to burnout.

NOW WHAT?

1. *Find Your Shard of Glass.* Discover what you're trying to prove, and to whom. Look for the chips on your shoulder and discard them. Look for the early symptoms of unhealthy, obsessive passion.
2. *Lead from Behind.* Instead of being the cheerleader-in-chief, allow for more stillness and silence in your leadership style.
3. *Stop Proving Yourself Right.* Too much passion causes leaders to take on new roles and big challenges simply to prove to themselves and others that they can do it. Get to know your own motivation, and avoid taking on opportunities just to show the world — or yourself — that your way is the right way.
4. *Start Proving Yourself Wrong.* Avoid the natural tendency to double down on an argument in the face of challenging evidence. Instead, reconsider your strongest points of view at work, and seek out data to help you see the other side.

5. *Stay Healthy with the Buddy System.* It's tough to self-diagnose obsessive passion, so ask for help. Leaders should ask a trusted work friend to help them decide if they need to take a break.

6. *Stay Out of Trouble with the Buddy System.* Obsessive passion can cause leaders to justify morally questionable decisions. In addition to policing yourself, police each other at work.

7. *Look Outside Yourself.* Instead of ruminating over what your passion is, start working on helping someone else. Being focused on the needs of others generates more long-term happiness and satisfaction than obsessing over what your unique interest is.

8

Backstage Onstage Preparation

Ajay, an analyst at a top investment bank, wowed clients with structured, reasoned thinking and elegant financial models. Eager to gain experience and solve novel problems, he was first to volunteer for projects and often voiced his desire to be challenged. Ajay's impressive work ethic made him a model employee and even attracted attention from the top. To honor Ajay's performance, his manager rewarded him with an unusually important assignment: Ajay would lead a pitch to a CEO in the tech industry who sought an investment bank to advise on the acquisition of a promising start-up. A disruptive entrant into the music industry, the start-up targeted for acquisition had little history of revenue and few comparable peers against which to be valued.

The case whetted Ajay's appetite for a complicated valuation challenge. Ajay built complex models backed by rigorous research to demonstrate the profit potential of the acquisition. He exhaustively prepared to defend his model, putting in hours upon hours of time to account for dozens of different future scenarios. Ajay felt the decision was a no-brainer: the tech firm should definitely acquire the start-up. "My work here is done," he thought. "Now I just have to say the words."

In the morning, Ajay showered, put on his best suit, and picked up a double-shot espresso, arriving at work ready to impress. The CEO greeted him with a firm handshake and subsequently unleashed the unexpected—a barrage of unconventional questions designed to get Ajay off his script. Would Ajay work for the start-up founder in question? What did Ajay make of the culture of the start-up? How would Ajay value the company as a talent acquisition? Ajay's preparation of his model had been so intense and thorough and his conclusions so compelling that he froze upon hearing the off-topic questions. Instead of responding to the CEO's inquiries, he rummaged through his notes and began blankly regurgitating his prepared conclusions. It was as if Ajay had become temporarily deaf, unable to listen and respond to his most important client. The CEO wanted Ajay to spar with him in conversation but Ajay's faculties had been hijacked by the inertia of his preparation.

A look of disappointment slowly flushed across the CEO's face. "It seems you're not prepared to have this conversation," the CEO suggested. He added, "Models are helpful to a point but they're only a prediction, part of the story. I need the whole story." And with that, he thanked Ajay for his time, shook his hand, and left.

Back at his desk, Ajay sat speechless. Unprepared? "I spent eighty hours working on that model. I crushed it," he thought. Due to the lackluster meeting, the CEO passed on hiring Ajay's bank to advise on the possible acquisition. Ajay was crestfallen. How had he been caught so off guard by the CEO? Why didn't the CEO even attempt to explore the model Ajay had prepared so exhaustively? Ajay's conclusions would have made even his toughest finance professor proud, and yet the CEO seemed uninterested and even flippant toward Ajay's thoughtful preparation. When preparation causes us to ignore the moment, stuck in our own heads, it backfires.

The Inertia of Preparation

Success comes to those who put in the hard work to prepare diligently. Want to play football on Sunday afternoon? Then prepare through the week, and throughout your life. Want to ace the job interview? Do your homework. If you're unprepared, you'll look unprofessional. No matter what the setting, leaders must be ready to add value. And readiness doesn't happen on its own. Invest the time before the sales meeting, product launch, courtroom trial, or press conference so you're ready for whatever comes. Preparation is obviously a virtue. What's less obvious is the way that certain approaches to preparation can stunt your growth, lower your performance, and limit your potential to advance in your career.

It's no wonder Ajay fell flat on his face in his meeting. Multiple forces conspire to junk up our mental models of preparation in the workplace, from sociology to education to culture to cognition. Erving Goffman, a sociologist, used the metaphor of a stage to describe human social interaction.[1] He shows that we're always onstage. But too often we imagine ourselves backstage, preparing for an event that will start at some point in the future. The truth is, everything we do, even preparation, is onstage. The event is life, and it's already started.

Goffman starts his metaphor by describing a particularly stressful event, a wedding. Of course there's happiness and joy, but for the bride and groom, there's often a bit of stress. Goffman explores the source of the wedding day stress, and he argues that it's much more than the enormity of the commitment. When you get married, there are people in the same room from many different aspects of your life—friends from high school, from college, and from work along with your closest family and some family members you see only occasionally. Each of these people sees a different version of you. You're not the same person with your Aunt Gladys as you are with Pat, your college friend. So when Pat and Gladys stand beside each other, which version of yourself should you be?

As Goffman argues, you're not stressed out because you've been fake to either Pat or Gladys. Presenting yourself as someone different to different people is a natural part of being human. Just as it's empathetic to adjust a message to an audience, it's a social norm to be different versions of yourself to different people. And it's stressful when so many different audiences are suddenly in the same room.

The point is, as long as we're awake and conscious, we're on stage, making choices about how we present ourselves. But sometimes we kid ourselves into thinking we're backstage, preparing for a show that's about to start. We're studying before a test or practicing before the play opens. The point of this chapter is to encourage you to embrace the fact that you're always on stage. Once you make that mental shift, it changes the way you prepare and raises your performance. The alternative approach, to vacillate between a relaxed, backstage, off-camera mindset sometimes and an intense, onstage, on-camera attitude at other times leads to unsustainable swings, lower performance, and fewer opportunities to learn.

But based on the way school works, you'd think backstage learning is the right way. With constant testing we become conditioned to equating responsible preparation with exhaustive memorization and independent analysis—the more the better. We cram information into our brains and spew it back out onto a multiple-choice test. It's natural to hold on to the mental model of preparation that made us successful as students. But the game has changed. We have to stop overpreparing and mispreparing for a test that will never come.

Other remnants of our schooling do harm as well. For example, the concept of academic specialization hurts us if we narrowly define our expertise as limited to our one field of study at the cost of cultivating complementary skills. A+ obsession, another trap, tricks leaders into preparing for the satisfaction of a mental A+. If you've ever graded yourself or others on their preparation, you may be a victim of this pernicious mania. Even diplomas can seductively whisper in our ear, "You've arrived. You're done learning." This is not to suggest diplomas aren't valuable or shouldn't be a source of deep pride. However, although diplomas help frame our future success, leaders must match knowledge with growth-oriented qualities like an appetite for constant learning, ability to take and learn from feedback, and a willingness to change one's mind.

In our youth, many of us participated in the Boy Scouts or Girl Scouts and can instantly recall the motto, "Be Prepared." We likely heard this adage as a voice egging us on to prepare more backstage. But Robert

Baden-Powell, founder of the scouting movement, described the motto as not just an activity of the mind, but of the body as well. In order to be prepared, one must approach a task holistically, thinking through possible scenarios and training the body so that when the moment comes to do your duty, you're conditioned to act. Baden-Powell built scouting around performance-based badges that pull students out of classrooms, books, and solitary learning and into the world to perform over a hundred different hands-on activities. The scouting model achieves true readiness not through disembodied study, but through integrated preparation that couples mind and body training with performance.

Before the Internet made shipping products and services an instant act, product development life cycles took years. In the old model, anything that hit the stores had to be polished. Now, crowds fund half-baked ideas through supportive communities, and Fortune 500 companies test product assumptions under the safe haven of "beta" status. As I pointed out in Chapter Five on excellence, in the recent Facebook IPO filing, founder Mark Zuckerberg included a section on "The Hacker Way" to reclaim the positive merits of the word "hacker." Zuckerberg describes it as "an approach to building that involves continuous improvement and iteration." But although norms are changing, many of us find it hard to let go of our impulse to fully bake everything.

A friend of mine landed a job at Google right out of college. An alien to Silicon Valley culture, she found herself in a strange world that challenged her notions of preparation. Before Google, she interned at a law firm for a boss who praised her exacting eye for detail and reverent regard for being right before speaking up. Google released incomplete work as beta products and generally regarded everything as an experiment to learn from. The philosophy was: why waste time getting it right instead of simply shipping it and getting it right in real time? At first, she watched, bewildered, convinced that the company was letting products and features ship before they were ready. Finally, she let go of her preconceptions, embraced quick execution, and joined the high-speed, just-ship-it attitude that has led to Google's impressive track record of rapid product introductions.

Our brains shape our preparation habits too. Roughly one in five Americans suffers from anxiety disorders, according to the National Institute of Mental Health. A 2001 Gallup poll found two in five Americans are afraid to speak in front of an audience.[2] Fear and anxiety originate from a place deep in our brains and many of us find that compulsive overpreparing quiets our protesting brains like Xanax. Overpreparation may be comforting, but it has unintended consequences. When we prepare to calm our nerves, we're slowly falling in love with our work in a way that makes us less open to feedback. Not to mention we waste time that could have been spent more productively.

A clue from a study on jazz and the brain hints at the neurological roots disconnecting preparation and performance. A pair of Johns Hopkins and government scientists examined the brains of six jazz pianists performing well-memorized C-scales and improvised tunes. They used MRIs to isolate blood flow patterns for each activity. In both scenarios, improvising (that is, going off script) resulted in reduced blood flow to the part of the brain linked to planned actions like self-censoring. At the same time, improvising increased blood flow to the part of the brain linked with self-expression and individuality. In other words, switching from prepared to improvised activity changed brain states.[3] The findings present an interesting trend and suggest that the brain actually does have to switch gears as it goes from prepared to improvised activity, at least in music.

Unless you take tests for a living, the predominant form of preparation in our culture does you no favors. Leaders must scrutinize and shift their mental model of preparation to maximize performance at work. Don't use preparation as a drug or a crutch.

All the World's a Stage

After college, I worked at Agnew, Carter, McCarthy Public Relations and had an opportunity to watch the magic of Jack Agnew, a partner and pitching pro, in action. My silver-tongued boss had as diverse and storied a career as they come, including singing backup to Elvis Presley in the late 1950s and hosting a children's television show in upstate New York. Full of charisma and authenticity, he mesmerized potential clients with effortlessly flowing wit, humor, and charm. Jack was a natural, or so I thought. On the day of an important pitch, I arrived at work early to prepare more, largely as a way to calm my nerves. For me, that would mean doing more research about the client's industry positioning. To my surprise, I heard my boss's voice, with characteristic energy and swagger, booming out of the conference room. "He got them in the conference room before 8 AM! Amazing," I thought. I craned my neck around the door and discovered my boss alone, practicing his pitch in his warm, conversational style. To me preparation equaled quiet research. But to Jack, preparation meant practicing as if the show had already started.

There is no backstage. Of course, Shakespeare "discovered" this secret to leadership over four hundred years ago when he wrote in *As You Like It* that "All the world's a stage."

What does onstage preparation look like? It looks a lot like play, which sees no stage and embraces the moment. Improv comedy has a great deal to teach business leaders. If you've ever watched *Whose Line Is It Anyway?* you've seen mindful play elevated to almost symphonic comedic harmony. Improv may appear at odds with preparation. After all, don't those comedians just wing it? Yes, and no. Improv relies on rules and skills. Done well, like anything else, it looks effortless. It also illuminates the right tension between being fully present and bringing your gifts to bear in a work situation.

The kind of play inherent in improv flourishes in the absence of judgment. William Hall, founder of BATS Improv in San Francisco, one of the nation's oldest and most successful improv companies, points out that the problem with judgment is that it pushes us "out of the present moment to the future or the past."[4] To combat leaving the present, one of improv's cardinal rules is "yes, and." "Yes, and" means accepting what has just been said and adding to it. In a business context, when you've done lots of backstage preparation to fill your head with "truth," it jacks up the connections you need to make with people. There's certainly a time to speak your truth. But there's also a time to shut up and listen for new truth. Before you ignore the "Yes, and" rule and deny someone else's point, make sure it's the right move. Responding with "Yes, and" allows you to learn more and build a bridge from another point to your own.

Hall, though, considers "Yes, and" to be a sacred cow of improv that deserves a bit of tipping. It's helpful language for those getting started, but the more essential point, as he puts it, is "move things forward." Moving things forward requires more judgment than simply repeating a phrase. Sometimes, it even involves saying "No." One of Hall's improv games is to ask students to move things forward in a scene by saying no instead of yes. The game helps students practice and develop a deeper level of onstage reaction.

It's probably not surprising that an improv comedian would be an exemplar of onstage preparation for business. A self-professed mediocre student growing up in North Hollywood, California, Adam Carolla preferred the football field over the classroom. Trying on a number of jobs after high school, including carpet cleaner, carpenter, boxing instructor, and traffic school instructor, he found that these jobs mismatched his talents and ambitions. But rather than complain, he dug in, building a muscle of doing things well and seeing all work as opportunity.

Weary from noncreative jobs and having always been appreciated for his sense of humor, Carolla pursued improv, learning with The Groundlings, a Los Angeles improv company. "I realized that I needed time onstage. I needed to learn all the techniques of comedy and improv...all the rules that are involved with it. They're invisible rules and if you do them well no one will know you're doing them well," Carolla observed during a guest lecture he gave at USC's Marshall School of Business. With "so many open mics to wait in line on," Carolla set to work performing. Carolla cherished experience, even when unpleasant or poorly compensated. Reflecting back on the early, low-paying comedy jobs he held, he suggests that he should have been paying them.

Carolla's foundation and opportunism rocketed him to success, though not without occasional, violent hiccups. Carolla cohosted the television show *Loveline*, and then his own radio show, *The Adam*

Carolla Show. But after three years, his syndicated radio program was abruptly canceled. Undeterred, Carolla started podcasting.

Within the first twenty-four hours of its release, fans downloaded the podcast two hundred and fifty thousand times. By the time the third podcast was released, *The Adam Carolla Show* had become the most downloaded podcast on iTunes in the United States and Canada. Two years later in May 2011, Carolla's podcast unseated Ricky Gervais's podcast to break the Guinness World Record for most downloaded podcast *ever*. Channeling the tools and the muscles he has developed over time into new situations, Carolla notes, "There's a new door opening every five minutes."

Carolla learned by doing and by doing well. He became an active student of his professions, improvising his way through opportunities but working hard throughout.

Seven Ideas to Take Your Preparation to Center Stage

While backstage preparation wastes time and energy, onstage preparation raises performance. To make this shift, you'll need to shed the school-based approach to preparing for life as if it's a test, and instead learn to practice with the intensity of a world-class athlete. Trust yourself to make it up as you go along, rely on your instincts more, and you can help start a movement of leaders learning from each other.

1. Troubleshoot Your Preparation Style

What is your mental model for preparation for work? Is it informed by the way you prepared for other, fundamentally different situations in life? Are you a crammer? Are you able to connect performance to preparation? Do you use preparation as an anxiety-reducer? Do you find a way to practice improvisation? Are you open to new ideas and throwing out agendas? Are you more prone to overprepare or underprepare?

I played the saxophone in high school and college, even considering becoming a professional musician for a time. The only problem with that plan was my lack of talent. Coming out of high school, I prepared intensely, spending hours battling swift staccato tempos and challenging phrases. In college, a professor observed that I clumsily shifted my fingers through awkward note progressions and muscled my way through lightning-fast transitions during practice. No amount of practice would help if I continued this way. I had it all wrong.

The key insight my professor shared was that my technique during practice formed bad habits. Rather than do battle against difficult phrases, I should slow the piece down to a tempo at which I could play the notes perfectly. For example, if I was learning a tricky phrase to be played at 144 beats per minute, I should slow the tempo down to say, 60 beats per minute. Then I played the difficult phrase with perfect technique at that rate three times. Then, and only then, could I increase the tempo of my metronome by the small increment of four beats per minute. Repeating this sequence twenty times enabled me to master the piece with perfect technique.

I suggest a little more perfectionism before the event, and a little less perfectionism during the event. During a prep for a sales pitch, say the words out loud that you plan to say in the meeting. Work with a partner and assume your first version will be bad. Slow it down and slowly perfect it. Then get ready to let it rip during the pitch.

My professor suggested that in addition to slowing pieces down and practicing with perfect technique, I should make practice more like performance by visualizing the concert hall and trying to elicit the feeling of performance. I made myself more nervous during practice, so concerts would seem less daunting. Learning of the damage that practicing with poor technique and not including mental preparation was having on my saxophone performance, I righted my preparation and elevated my play to an entirely new level. I hit my personal limit, maxing my potential. Sometimes the way we practice can wreak havoc on our performance. Practice alone gives no assurances. Rather, perfect practice makes perfect.

Reflecting on and classifying your current approach is a critical first step. Jamie, a young, talented biotech professional, realized the flaw in her preparation strategy for public speaking after keynoting a biotech conference. Despite a willingness to take on bold new challenges and opportunities, Jamie suffered from anxiety around public speaking. Ever determined to overcome such a challenge, she enthusiastically accepted the invitation to keynote a conference. She didn't get the opportunity to speak to five hundred people every day.

With several months until the big day, Jamie practiced constantly. She wrote her speech, made elegant slides, set about memorizing key points and transitions and practiced until she was blue in the face. Feeling a destructive anxiety rise within her whenever she thought about her upcoming task, she would rehearse repeatedly to her empty living room each night and over the weekends, for hours on end, until she felt a sense of relief physiologically. The day of the conference finally came. As Jamie approached the podium, crushing anxiety filled her body. She made it through the speech, tripping over words and barely managing to save transitions. Hardly able to remember the thirty minutes and thoroughly exhausted, Jamie thought about what happened.

Anxiety drove Jamie's approach. She thought repeated practice would make all the difference, but it didn't. Instead, she needed to be aware of the role anxiety played in her preparation and find ways to channel the anxiety, whether that was meeting with a professional to look into alternative therapies, getting real world public speaking practice in a supportive and low-risk environment, or finding positive ways to productively reduce anxiety. Because she gained insight into her tendencies toward anxiety-driven preparation, Jamie joined Toastmasters, an educational nonprofit that helps people improve their public speaking skills, to get more speaking practice, and she began looking into cognitive therapies to prevent debilitating anxiety in the future.

2. Learn by Doing

A 1999 *Journal of the American Medical Association* (JAMA) study tested assumptions about continuing medical education (CME) and arrived at some surprising and powerful insights about optimal preparation for doctors. Physicians spend an average of fifty hours per year in CME activities "ostensibly geared toward improving their performance and optimizing the outcomes of their patients." Yet many of these classes don't do anything to improve a doctor's ability to take care of patients.

To determine whether performance improved, JAMA reviewed sixteen studies of the effect of continued learning on physician performance. They classified the approaches as three different types—didactic, interactive, and mixed methods. The didactic methods were lectures, presentations. or printed materials. The interactive approach included workshops, small-group work. and individualized training sessions. Mixed CME included elements of both.

Of the studies reviewed analyzing didactic CME methods, none had a measurable effect on physician performance. Interestingly, however, the vast majority of studies analyzing both interactive and mixed CME methods had a significant positive effect on physician practice. In other words, when continuing education included interactive elements, physician performance improved, but when those elements weren't there, physician performance did not improve. Given the tremendous investment of time and resources going into CME, the study findings encourage doctors to seek out interactive learning.[5] On the one hand, it's not a surprise that the interactive approach is more effective. But keep in mind that thousands of doctors satisfy their CME requirements every year through purely passive learning methods that produce no improvement in patient outcome.

I hate this ass-covering approach to preparation. You tick the box that says "CME credit complete," and you move on. I've seen the same lazy approach way too many times in the world of corporate education. Mandatory training programs that merely broadcast information waste time. But worse than wasting time, they give learning a bad name. Skeptical employees can simply point to the vast array of time-sucking, energy-depleting, soul-draining compulsory education and make the case that the only way to learn to do the job is on the job. That's not true, of course. Training programs that re-create the same intensity and nuance of the job can increase your team's readiness in a safer way with more opportunities for reflection and growth. But I don't blame the skeptics. They've got enough evidence to make their case that training sucks. Let's try not to make it easy for them, though. If you can invest the time and money it takes to make training that actually simulates the job, do it. Otherwise, don't bother.

3. Hold (Moot) Court

If you've never participated in a moot court, you're not alone. The practice exemplifies the kind of simulated performance that can help leaders improve performance more actively and, arguably, effectively than reading a book. James, an accomplished tax attorney in Washington, D.C., holds mock trials, simulated oral arguments, to prepare for each case he argues. He describes the process as intensely interactive and iterative. Whenever an important trial approaches, he holds four to five moot courts to practice arguments. Often, the court is composed of his colleagues, but he also invites experts to come and tear apart his team's arguments.

James notes that the way they argue a case changes dramatically from the first to the last moot court. They gain invaluable insights and along the way have an opportunity to test out specific arguments, simulate being in front of the judge, prepare for questioning, and gain a comfortable familiarity with their argument. He stresses that the process of performing his argument in a realistic test environment is critical to shaping his argument and gaining confidence in his message.

Think back to Ajay's story. Introducing a recurring form of simulated client interaction into his toolbox could help him avoid experiences like the one with the CEO. Although law schools now have moot court clubs and competitions, it's interesting to remember that they didn't for forty years. Students brought back this interactive preparation tool. The onus is on us as leaders, then, to create our own moot courts.

4. Pretotype

The year is 1970 and you're in a conference room in upstate New York. Ashtrays pepper the table and smoke rings emanate from serious expressions. A debate rages. IBM, in the business of typewriters and computers, has a decision to make. Personal computers haven't taken off in the mass market and keyboards are a major culprit. Thirty years ago, most managers didn't type. Typing proficiency, or lack thereof, blocked the way to mass market adoption.

Abuzz about a new technology concept, the room fractures around opinion. The technology that could change the game? Voice recognition. If IBM developed speech-to-text technology, typewriters would no longer be needed. Early focus groups loved the idea. What could be easier than speaking? Development will be challenging and costly. Investing the amount of money needed into research and development would effectively be betting the company on the success of voice recognition technology. Should they do it? What would you do? Will people behave like they say they will and buy the technology?

Legend has it that because they couldn't afford to make it, IBM came up with a most clever solution to test out the concept. They invited a focus group to come in and had them dictate to a computer. In an adjoining room, a super-typist instantaneously typed the testers' words. The group of testers, previously enthusiastic about the idea, found that in reality, dictating to a computer made their throats sore, was noisy, and was inappropriate for confidential or sensitive messages. Through early testing, IBM made the wise decision not to move forward with the technology.

Alberto Savoia, serial entrepreneur, retells this story to describe an idea he calls "pretotyping," a more memorable variant of "pretend-o-typing." Before spending the money to develop a prototype, IBM found a tremendously low-cost way to test user interest and saved time and money. "Make sure you're building the right 'it' before you build 'it' right," Savoia advises. Translating IBM's pretotyping wisdom to preparation for leaders, leaders know the value of getting feedback early when preparing. Next time you have a big work task to do, find a quick and dirty way to figure out what would actually be valuable work and save doing it well for when you have the "right 'it.'"[6]

5. Practice with Intensity

Adam Nelson is an unlikely shot put champion. Shot put, a track and field event that entails hurling a sixteen-pound metal ball as far as possible, favors the behemoth. Generously measured at six feet tall, Nelson is short by shot put standards, typically the shortest competitor on the field. For example, Christian Cantwell, one of Nelson's competitors, stands five inches taller and outweighs him by nearly eighty pounds. And unlike most elite track and field stars, Nelson earned an Ivy League degree, majoring in government at Dartmouth during his training. And yet, Nelson has won two Olympic silver medals and one world championship in track and field. Part of Nelson's improbable success can be attributed to the intensity he brings to his preparation. Instead of conserving energy for the big events, he exerts tremendous bursts of energy during practice. His goal isn't conservation — it's simulation. "When preparing for a high stress, unique situation," he said, "you want to simulate as many possible variations of the scenario as you can. Most of the time when people fail in performances, it's because they failed to simulate all of the scenarios beforehand."[7]

To plan for training, he maps out the most important competition of the year and works backward. Nelson's plan of preparation also includes key nutrition, mental preparation, sleep, and social targets. Nelson knows himself well and through awareness and intention prepares with his whole life in mind for optimal performance so that when a performance arrives, he's ready.

Another element particular to Nelson's preparation takes place just before he steps into the shot put ring. To psych himself up for each throw, Nelson follows a choreographed routine each time he throws. Jumping up and down, Nelson yanks off his warm-up sweats, yells like a crazy person and stomps into the ring with deep focus. This routine becomes a signal to his body that it's time to perform and encourages a desirable physiological response. He goes through this exact sequence each time he practices. Actors also use similar sorts of cues, that they often call anchors, to signal their body that a performance is about to begin. Importantly, they use these anchors before a dress rehearsal as well.

Leaders would be wise to borrow the trick of developing a consistent routine and practicing with the same intensity they hope to bring to their performance at work. In the big moments, like giving an important speech, I want leaders to relax more. But in the little moments, like when they're putting together their notes for the speech, I want leaders to relax less. Raise your game during practice and you'll raise your game during performance.

6. Be More Human

Nick Morgan, CEO of Public Words and author of *Trust Me: Four Steps to Authenticity and Charisma*, believes that public speaking instruction is done all wrong. As an executive communications coach, Morgan previously taught the mechanics of public speaking—how to hold your hands, distribute eye contact, move through the space to engage your audience, and the like. But then Morgan realized this approach had an unintended consequence.[8]

By focusing on getting all of the mechanics of giving a talk right, presenters introduce an almost imperceptible, but real lag. Your brain says, "Eye contact. Make a gesture." Meanwhile, your audience sees stiffness and inauthenticity. A better approach, argues Morgan, is to start instead by thinking of which emotion you hope to convey. And then you need to feel that emotion yourself. To feel that emotion, mix in a little visualization. For example, if you want to feel open and vulnerable in front of the audience, think of a person with whom you delight in being open. Practice this technique before a speech or high-stakes conversation. After the talk, you may not remember doing anything specific to signal openness with your gestures or voice, but based on Morgan's research of video-taping thousands of speakers, it's likely that there were dozens of subtle signals you gave that relaxed you and your audience.

Whenever I give a keynote, I start by looking at pictures of my girls doing something silly. My first job as a speaker is to engage the audience, and I have good luck doing that with a smile. I want the audience to be glad they're there, and I need to be happy about it myself first. Taking a glimpse at a picture of Margaret putting rabbit ears behind Emily's head while Emily gives a too-cool-to-care scowl makes me smile, every time. I think this higher-level approach to giving a presentation that Morgan advocates has wide relevance beyond the world of giving speeches.

There are lists of tips and tricks to do anything you want to do at work. And if you're doing rote, mechanical work with the same repeatable process, then tips and tricks are great. But increasingly, software does the rote work, which means that we humans had better be good at the thing software can't do so well, yet: authentic, human interaction. The problem with filling your head up with a list of tips and tricks is that your brain becomes a computer database and you lose your ability to listen and react in the moment. Raise your leadership up to the level of human intent and then let the mechanics follow. Think about the moments of truth in your work week. Whether it's a client visit, a team meeting, or a pitch to investors, focus on the human goals. What feelings do you want to engender? Do what it takes to get those feelings felt. If you want your client to trust you, for example, then one week you might need to provide detailed analytics; the next week you might need to share a personal story; and the week after that you might need to give some advice. No checklist of client meetings is going to help you as much as a high-level focus on the feeling you need to engender, and a trust in your own human ability to generate that feeling in someone else.

7. Apprentice Each Other

Eighty-five-year-old Jiro Ono believes that the key to success as a sushi chef is to "dedicate your life to mastering this skill." That's good news for the lucky few who get to eat sushi at his ten-seat restaurant, considered by food experts like Anthony Bourdain to be the best spot in the world to enjoy the Japanese delicacy. But the news is more mixed for Ono's son, Yoshikazu, who at fifty-one continues to study under his father. The 2012 documentary *Jiro Dreams of Sushi* shows how heavily the weight of working to live up to his father's standards sits on Yoshikazu's shoulders. Apprenticeship is an ancient method of learning with thousands of years of history in which a student patiently learns from a master. But today, with expertise more distributed, there are more efficient ways of learning. Instead of the slow, deliberate path of gathering deep expertise from a master like Jiro Ono, we can apprentice each other through open, crowd-sourced learning.

Want to write a novel? Join the "National Novel Writing Month" community in any November. This event, run by the nonprofit Office of Letters and Light, serves as a support group and a community of practice. It encourages people who've considered writing a novel to finally get on it with it. In November 2011, more than thirty-six thousand people finished writing a novel of at least fifty-thousand words. As it says on the month-long event's website: "You will be writing a lot of crap. And that's a good thing. By forcing yourself to write so intensely, you are giving yourself permission to make mistakes. To forgo the endless tweaking and editing and just create. To build without tearing down."[9] Sometimes the final product doesn't end up as crap, though. Sara Gruen wrote the first draft of her *New York Times* best-selling novel, *Like Water for Elephants*, during the event in 2007.[10]

Many others have gone on to publish their novels. But for most of the first-time novelists the primary benefits are the intense learning that comes only from letting your guard down, and the rush that comes from completing a tough task like climbing a mountain or completing a marathon. Aspiring filmmakers have a similar opportunity, in an even more dramatically time-compressed event. The 48-Hour Film Project asks teams to make a film in a weekend. As they say, "While the time limit places an unusual restriction on the filmmakers, it is also liberating by putting an emphasis on doing instead of talking."[11]

If you're the expert, resist the urge to transfer your knowledge in the slow, steady drip of apprenticeship. Even if that's the way you were taught, perhaps you can create or find an opportunity for people to learn from and teach each other as they do something significant. We admire the lifelong dedication of masters like sushi chef Jiro Ono. Let's also appreciate the accomplishments of a movement of apprentices who serve no master except each other.

Conclusion

Ajay's bad day at the beginning of the chapter *could* be judged as a failed performance. But in a world of onstage preparation, failures are repurposed as gifts, the "yes, and" suggestion of an ever-present audience. If your whole life is onstage, then your whole life is backstage. In other words, making all of life preparation renders every moment an opportunity to learn and grow. Real time is the only time. Everything else is memory or imagination. This moment, right now, is the only one that exists for sure. Live in it more fully, more openly, and more bravely, and you'll never stop growing.

Preparation becomes a sacred cow for leaders when they hide out and study, polishing slides for hours on end, falling in love with their own ideas. Instead, I urge leaders to take their ideas out into the world right now and get messy and learn and grow in the process. Leaders who make themselves vulnerable to prepare during work instead of before work are richly rewarded. Cut the curtain and enter the adventure of life onstage.

Putting It into Practice

WHAT IS ONSTAGE PREPARATION?

Onstage preparation means getting better at something while doing it, instead of getting better at something before doing it. The key to honoring preparation as a value in the world of work is to remember that life is not a test to be passed, but a single, integrated performance.

SO WHAT?

Too much preparation before work can waste time, cause leaders to fall in love with their work, worsen listening skills, and dilute a leader's presence. With an attitude of constant testing, constant tweaking, and constant learning, the work itself becomes the best preparation.

NOW WHAT?

1. *Troubleshoot Your Preparation Style.* Unhelpful mental models and cognition often cloud your practice of preparation. Look for patterns in your past for clues that you may be overpreparing out of habit or as a means of lowering your anxiety.
2. *Learn by Doing.* When you make time for training and learning, make sure that you create an environment that simulates the real work.
3. *Hold (Moot) Court.* Low-stakes feedback is critical to top performance but may not be readily available. Be creative in finding ways to simulate performance as a standard part of your preparation.
4. *Pretotype.* It's easy for leaders to get sucked into spending more time than needed on things no one cares about. Find quick and dirty ways to get feedback early on so you only spend time on things that add value.
5. *Practice with Intensity.* Leaders do not often exploit mental preparation. Tools like holistic planning, triggering routines, and visualization augment other forms of preparation for world-class performance.
6. *Be More Human.* Overly focusing on mechanics in preparation can make you robotic in performance. When you get stuck in mechanics, channel your efforts to intent and emotion instead, and let the mechanics follow.
7. *Apprentice Each Other.* Instead of the deliberate, slow process of passing down expertise from master to apprentice, build an open, crowd-sourced community of apprentices learning from each other.

9

Extinguish Your Backfires

Before you ever did anything, thought anything, or believed anything, you sensed something. Inside your mother's womb you started the life-long work of making sense of the world. You've spent your entire life constructing meaning out of the details you perceive. At first, it's physical. As a baby you learned the response that crying would get. As a toddler you learned how it felt to bump your head on a corner.

As you became an adolescent you began to make fundamental choices about how to perceive the world. Is it hard work or luck that pays off? Is life fair? Is it better to stand out or fit in? As you became an adult and entered the workplace, you made choices about how to perceive the world of work. Are excellence and balance the secret to your success? Is it always a good idea to collaborate? Once you've made a choice of how to perceive the world, you've put on a pair of glasses that alters your perception. Remember that those glasses are a choice. I don't know what glasses you've decided to wear. The question is: do you?

In 2005, the novelist David Foster Wallace gave the commencement speech at Kenyon College. Given that Wallace was considered to be one of the great writers of his generation, it's not a surprise that this commencement address has been identified as one of the most powerful. He started the speech with a quick story: "Two young fish swim along and meet an older fish swimming the other way. The older fish nods at the youngsters and says 'Morning, boys. How's the water?' The two young fish swim on for a bit, and then one of them looks over at the other and asks 'What the hell is water?'"[1]

Wallace urged the graduating students not to live an unconscious life of default existence, but to do the hard work of purposefully becoming aware of the world. Although this is hard for new graduates, it's even harder for mature professionals. The more you espouse virtues without questioning them, the harder it gets to see when they've become sacred cows. We humans naturally become more and more like the humans we surround ourselves with. And if we're in a culture that doesn't challenge our sacred cows, without a doubt, it's tough to get perspective. The job of this book has been to help you get that perspective.

How you construct meaning is the single most important act of leadership that you can make. No other choice affects so much. Every thought, belief, and action you make is affected by the way you perceive the world. When you see the world through "new ideas are better than old ideas" glasses, you selectively filter in and filter out part of existence. There are consequences to that decision, so make sure you've thoughtfully decided which glasses you wear. The journey of this book has been to help you see that you have that choice, and to help you make that choice.

It's not easy to spot sacred cows, even for experts in leadership. Byron Hanson, one of my friends and colleagues from Duke CE, is a Canadian scholar of leadership who has lived on and off in Australia, his wife's native country. In 2004, Byron and three friends of his, each of whom was also recognized as an expert in leadership, set out on a five-day walk through the Fitzgerald River National Park, which cuts through the rugged bush country of Western Australia. It was an adventure they'd been planning for over a year, and the four fit guys in their thirties were eager to tackle the challenge. They geared up with forty-pound packs of food, camping equipment, water, and water storage (as there would be no sources of water on the trek). They also carried a satellite phone as there is no mobile coverage in the Fitzgerald. They pushed their way through with optimism. They had planned well, including water drops that had been strategically left at certain spots along the trek by a support person a few days earlier. There was no path, and each step was a plodding exercise in fighting through prickly bushes, stepping on and over loose rocks the size of soccer balls, all while staying alert for signs of dehydration and snakes. They kept trudging along, but at a slower pace than they'd planned when they scheduled their water drops.

On day two as the sun set, they flipped on their headlamps to see their way along the vast sand dunes that hug the isolated coastline of the park. They should have reached their first water drop four hours earlier. One of Byron's friends, Troy Hendrickson, who now teaches with Byron at Curtin Graduate School of Business in Perth, Australia, noted that they'd only been able to cover 1 km/hour for the previous eight consecutive hours due to the harshness of the terrain — much slower than their plan.

"What was unsaid was unbelievable," said Byron. After the four proud men finished the last of their water and the temperature began to plummet, the anxiety rose, but no one spoke. Finally, after a few frantic calls on the satphone with the park ranger to get some bearings, just before midnight they stumbled onto their water source and pitched a hurried camp for the night. Exhausted, they studied their map and determined an early start would be required if they were to make the next water drop the following day. "It was all about the plan," Byron recalled. "Even though we were exhausted and behind our schedule, we just stuck to the plan." The next day, about five hours in, it was becoming clear that the hikers were not going to make the next water drop and again no one was saying anything. They just continued to labor through the thick bush. And then Gavin Rainbow, the most inexperienced hiker in the group, said something that proved to be the turning point. As the group was looking at the map and trying to find a way to the next water source, he said: "You know, we could just go back."

"That simple comment made us all pause," remembers Byron. "We never even thought about going back or about even thinking of an alternative way out until that moment. We had our heads down driving to a destination and were not willing to see other options." So in that moment the group finally opened up to their reality, changed course, and found their way out safely.

"Our journey ended up being more about exploring our egos than Australian bush," said Byron. "And the irony was, these topics were what I was right in the middle of studying for my Ph.D." Byron and the boys couldn't see the nature of their challenges because they were blinded by their sacred cows. They needed a new way of seeing the world.

For them, their sacred cows were completion, follow-through, and masculine adventure. Inside the workplace, we don't have freezing temperatures and parched mouths to lets us know we're in danger. The sacred cows at the workplace do their damage in a more subtle way.[2]

As a leader, you may know someone who has fallen prey to the power of one of the seven virtues turned sacred cows that I have described in this book. Use the steps revealed in the chapters to help that other person recognize the unintended consequences of their choice.

But the most fundamental use of this book is to help you recognize which is your own biggest sacred cow. As you identify the virtues that backfire for you, you'll come face-to-face with your own values. Spend some time reflecting on how you came to hold them. Think about your most beloved relative and what you learned from that person. Consider your favorite thinkers, your political party, or your religion. Reflect on your deepest beliefs, formed when you were young. It's likely that the virtues you hold most closely are there for deep and personal reasons.

Keep them. Those virtues are your babies, and they shouldn't be thrown out with the bathwater. The goal isn't for you to change who you are or what you believe. The goal is to stay true to yourself while avoiding the ways your unexamined beliefs and automatic behaviors can backfire.

Even worse than not examining them, some leaders are so proud of their beliefs that it's impossible for them to imagine how they might be anything other than virtuous. An executive at the large defense contractor I mentioned in Chapter Five told me a story that shows how the virtues we're proudest of might contain the most hidden dangers. The executive had served in the Air Force, and he described a colonel who had been the commanding officer (C.O.) of the first base where he had been stationed after graduating from the Academy. The C.O. of that base cared deeply about each airman who served under him and was viewed as one of the best leaders in the entire force. The C.O. took the unusual step of personally greeting each new arrival to base. "Even the most junior airman deserves my personal gratitude for his service," he said.

When the popular colonel retired, the troops were disappointed and skeptical that a new C.O. could ever be as popular. And they were right. Among the unpopular initiatives the new C.O. started: he recorded a video of himself that was played to welcome new airmen. No more personal greetings from the C.O. Each arriving airman was welcomed instead by a sergeant and a videotape.

After several months of wondering, the executive, at the time only a young man, mustered the courage to ask the new C.O. why he had replaced the personal greeting with a video recording. "I'm giving the sergeants a little bit of sunshine," said the new C.O. "I get enough as it is."

By raising the profile and importance of the more junior officers — in essence, the middle managers — and by diminishing his own role, the new C.O. instilled a culture at the base that didn't depend on a cult of his own personality. Though he never became as popular as his predecessor, the junior officers were more popular, respected, and empowered than they had ever been before.

The old C.O. was proud of taking the time to provide a personal welcome and thank you to each airman. He enjoyed being thought of as "one of the guys," and he detested his colleagues who played up the pomp and circumstance associated with senior officers. But his virtuous humility undermined his middle managers' attempts to establish their own importance in the chain of command. The beloved C.O. spent his entire career blinded to the unintended consequence of what he had perceived to be his greatest virtue.

You're likely proud of your own belief system. Each of the virtues I describe in this book has passed the test of time. But you must also be careful of the unintended consequences of these virtues — the damage that can be done in their names when they remain unexamined. That's the trick: keep the good while avoiding the unintended bad effects.

Find your biggest sacred cow. It's the water in David Foster Wallace's story that the fish swam in every day, unaware. If you work in a highly cooperative culture, then automatic collaboration could be your water. If you need to prove yourself to someone else, then you might be swimming in a sea of obsessive passion. Can't accept anything less than the best? You might be drowning in a pool of process excellence.

Think about your core beliefs. What's the advice you give? Your sacred cows may be hidden there, holding you back. Once you look for them, you'll start seeing them everywhere. You'll see them everywhere not because the world has changed, but because you've changed your way of perceiving the world.

Notes

Chapter One

1. Klaus Abbink and Abdolkarim Sadrieh, "The Pleasure of Being Nasty," *Economics Letters*, 105, no. 3 (December 2009): 306–308.

2. C. Seguin-Levesque, M.L.N. Laliberte, L. G. Pelletier, C. Blanchard, and R. J. Vallerand, "Harmonious and Obsessive Passion for the Internet: Their Associations with the Couple's Relationship," *Journal of Applied Social Psychology*, 33, Part 1 (2003): 197–221.

3. Emerald Archer, "You Shoot Like a Girl: Stereotype Threat and Marksmanship Performance in the U.S. Marine Corps." Paper presented at Western Political Science Association 2010 Annual Meeting.

4. Ba.Da Satoskar, *Gomantak: Prakruti ani Sanskruti, khand ek (in Marath)* (Pune: Sharda 1982): 20–21.

5. Clayton M. Christensen, *The Innovator's Dilemma: When New Technologies Cause Great Firms to Fail* (Boston: Harvard Business School Press, 1997).

6. M. T. Hansen, *Collaboration: How Leaders Avoid the Traps, Create Unity, and Reap Big Results* (Boston: Harvard Business School Press, 2009).

7. D. Jablonski, "Stephen Jay Gould 1941–2002," *American Scientist* 90, no. 4 (2002): 368.

8. Stephen J. Gould, *Full House: The Spread of Excellence from Plato to Darwin* (New York: Harmony Press, 1996).

9. G. Tabibnia, A. B. Satpute, and M. D. Lieberman, "The Sunny Side of Fairness: Preference for Fairness Activates Reward Circuitry (and Disregarding Unfairness Activates Self-Control Circuitry)," *Psychological Science*, 19 (2008): 339–347.

10. V. Gallese and A. Goldman, "Mirror Neurons and the Simulation Theory of Mind-Reading," *Trends in Cognitive Sciences* 2, no. 12 (December, 1998): 493–501.

11. D. L. Adler and J. Kounin, "Some Factors Operating at the Moment of Resumption of Interrupted Tasks," *Journal of Psychology*, 7 (1939): 355–367; M. Henle and G. Aull, "Factors Decisive for Resumption of Interrupted Activities: The Question Reopened," *Psychological Review*, 60 (1953): 81–88; K. Lewin, "Behavior and Development as a Function of the Total Situation," in *Manual of Child Psychology*, ed. L. Carmichael (New York: Wiley, 1946).

12. T. L. Juillerat, "The Usefulness or Uselessness of Novelty: Re-examining Assumptions About the Relationships Between Creativity and Innovation." Unpublished doctoral dissertation, Department of Organizational Behavior, University of North Carolina at Chapel Hill, 2010.

13. Marie McKendall, Helen Klein, Nancy Levenburg, and Denise de la Rosa, "College Student Cheating and Perceived Instructor Fairness," *Journal of the Academy of Business Education* 11 (Fall 2010): 14–32.

14. Michael Peters, Bryan Kethley, and Kimball Bullington, "The Relationship Between Homework and Performance in an Introductory Operations Management Course," *Journal of Education for Business* 77, no. 6 (July/August 2002): 340.

Chapter Two

1. Barry Schwartz, "The Tyranny of Choice," *Scientific American Mind* (December 2004).

2. A. Chernev, "The Dieter's Paradox," *Journal of Consumer Psychology* 21, no. 2 (April 2011): 178–183.

3. Decio Coviello, Andrea Ichino, and Nicola G. Persico, "Don't Spread Yourself Too Thin: The Impact of Task Juggling on Workers' Speed of Job Completion," IZA Discussion Paper No. 5280.

4. J. Chatman and J. Kennedy, "Psychological Perspectives on Leadership." In *Handbook of Leadership Theory and Practice: An HBS Centennial*

Colloquium on Advancing Leadership, eds. N. Nohria and R. Khurana (Boston: Harvard Business Press, 2010).

5. J. Collins and M. T. Hansen, *Great by Choice, Uncertainty, Chaos, and Luck — Why Some Thrive Despite Them All* (New York: HarperBusiness, 2011).

6. Teresa Amabile and S. Kramer, *The Progress Principle* (Boston: Harvard Business School Publishing, 2011).

7. Mayo Clinic Staff, "Rev Up Your Workout with Interval Training." http://www.mayoclinic.com/health/interval-training/SM00110/Retrieved September 21, 2012

8. Chatman and Kennedy, "Psychological Perspectives on Leadership."

9. P. Saffo, "Six Rules for Effective Forecasting," *Harvard Business Review* (July/August 2007).

10. C. Nemeth and M. Ormiston, "Creative Idea Generation: Harmony Versus Stimulation," *European Journal of Social Psychology* 37, no. 3 (2007): 524–535.

11. J. Collins, "Best New Year's Resolution? A 'Stop Doing' List," *USA Today* (December 30, 2003).

12. R. Martin, *Opposable Mind, Winning Through Integrative Thinking* (Boston: Harvard Business School Press, 2010).

Chapter Three

1. Jeff Zeleny, "Obama Gets a Thumbs-Up for His BlackBerry," *The Caucus: The Politics and Government Blog of The Times* (January 22, 2009). http://thecaucus.blogs.nytimes.com/2009/01/22/obama-gets-a-thumbs-up-for-his-blackberry/

2. C. Spiering, "Forget the BlackBerry, Obama Is Now the iPad President," *Washington Examiner* (August 8, 2012).

3. J. Castaldo, "How Management Has Failed at RIM," *Canadian Business* (January 19, 2012).

4. "Worst CEOs: A Check Up from the Head Up," narrated by Linda Werthheimer. "Morning Edition," *NPR* (December 27, 2011). http://www.npr.org/2011/12/27/144306969/worst-ceos-a-check-up-from-the-head-up

5. M. T. Hansen, *Collaboration: How Leaders Avoid the Traps, Create Unity, and Reap Big Results* (Boston: Harvard Business School Press, 2009).

6. Mark de Rond, *There Is an I in Team: What Elite Athletes and Coaches Really Know About High Performance* (Boston: Harvard Business Review Press, 2012).

7. Daily Beast, "Plywood Leadership with Gen. Stanley McChrystal," YouTube video. http://www.youtube.com/watch?v=EOFcXpFE3KU

Chapter Four

1. T. Haight, "Dr. Staffan Ericsson, President and CEO, Vivo Software," *Network Computing* (September, 1995). http://www.networkcomputing .com/611/611ntdericsson.html

2. H. Tabuchi, "How the Tech Parade Passed Sony By," *New York Times* (April 14, 2012).

3. Teresa Amabile, "Creativity and Innovation in Organizations," *Harvard Business Review*, HBS No. 9–396–239 (January 5, 1996). http://hbr.org /product/creativity-and-innovation-in-organizations/an/396239-PDF -ENG?

4. Personal interview.

5. Daniel Read and George Loewenstein, "Diversification Bias: Explaining the Discrepancy in Variety Seeking Between Combined and Separated Choices," *Journal of Experimental Psychology: Applied* 1, no. 1 (March 1995): 34–49.

6. Ibid., 49.

7. J. A. Goncalo, F. J. Flynn, and S. H. Kim (2010), "From a Mirage to an Oasis: Narcissism, Perceived Creativity, and Creative Performance." Retrieved July 30, 2012, from Cornell University, ILR School site: http://digitalcommons.ilr.cornell.edu/articles/309/

8. Dan Ariely, *The Upside of Irrationality* (New York: Harper, 2010).

9. Stephen King, *On Writing: A Memoir of the Craft* (New York: Scribner, 2000).

10. C. Heath and D. Heath, "The Myth About Creation Myths," *Fast Company* (March 1, 2007).

11. K. Kelly, *What Technology Wants* (New York: Viking, 2010).

12. T. Long, "Synecdoche: Compelling Complexity," *The Detroit News* (November 21, 2008).

13. B. Snyder, *Save the Cat* (Studio City, CA: Michael Wiese Productions, 2005).

14. J. S. Mueller, S. Melwani, and J. A. Goncalo, "The Bias Against Creativity: Why People Desire but Reject Creative Ideas," *Psychological Science* (in press).

15. John Tierney, "What's New? Exuberance for Novelty Has Benefits," *The New York Times* (February 13, 2012).

Chapter Five

1. J. Kramer, *Lombardi: Winning Is the Only Thing* (New York: Maddick Manuscripts, 1970).

2. O. Harari, *The Powell Principles: 24 Lessons from Colin Powell, a Legendary Leader* (New York: McGraw-Hill, 2002).

3. T. Harford, *Adapt: Why Success Always Starts with Failure* (New York: Farrar, Straus and Giroux, 2011).

4. Clayton M. Christensen, *The Innovator's Dilemma: When New Technologies Cause Great Firms to Fail* (Boston: Harvard Business School Press, 1997).

5. Tom Peters, Twitter post, August 7, 2012, 2:07 P.M., http://twitter.com /tom_peters

6. J. Jacobs, "Watson Triumphs on a Day That Had It All," *Hartford Courant* (June 28, 2010).

7. E. Catmull, "How Pixar Fosters Creativity," *Harvard Business Review* (September 2008).

8. "Pixar and Collective Creativity." Narrated by Paul Michelman. Harvard Business Review Ideacast (August 28, 2008). http://blogs.hbr.org /ideacast/2008/08/harvard-business-ideacast-109.html

9. C. Steele, "A Threat in the Air: How Stereotypes Shape Intellectual Identity and Performance," *American Psychologist* 52, no. 6 (June 1997): 613–629.

10. T. Dee, "Stereotype Threat and the Student-Athlete," NBER Working Paper No. 14705. Issued in February 2009.

11. Emerald Archer, "You Shoot Like a Girl: Stereotype Threat and Marksmanship Performance in the U.S. Marine Corps," paper presented at Western Political Science Association 2010 Annual Meeting.

12. N. Laporte, "Don't Know How? Well, Find Someone Who Does," *New York Times* (November 26, 2011).

13. "Wonder Kids," *Inventors Digest* (December 2010). http://www .inventorsdigest.com/archives/5267

14. Dennis Waitley, *The Psychology of Winning* (New York: Berkley Books, 1986).

15. Reid Hoffman, South by Southwest Interactive Conference, March 2011. http://venturebeat.com/2011/03/15/reid-hoffman-10-rules-of-entrepreneurship/

16. Zuckerberg, Mark, "Letter from Mark Zuckerberg in Facebook IPO Filing," *The Wall Street Journal MarketWatch* (February 1, 2012). http://articles.marketwatch.com/2012-02-01/industries/31028974_1_people-relationships-society

17. Often attributed to Hemingway, but I found it described as an old English aphorism in Thomas Longworth, *Longworth's American Almanac* (New York: T. Longworth, 1826).

18. Adam Horowitz, David Jacobson, Tom McNichol, and Owen Thomas, "101 Dumbest Moments in Business," *Business 2.0* (Jan/Feb 2007).

19. Baba Shiv, "The Art of the Imperfect Pitch" (August 27, 2012). Retrieved September 21, 2012, from http://www.gsb.stanford.edu/news/research/the-art-of-the-imperfect-pitch.html

20. Karl Weick, *The Social Psychology of Organizing* (New York: McGraw-Hill Humanities, 1979).

21. HBR Ideacast, "The Hidden Demons of High Achievers," podcast, *Harvard Business Review Blog Network* (May 26, 2011). http://blogs.hbr.org/ideacast/2011/05/the-hidden-demons-of-high-achi.html

22. Allan Metcalf, *OK: The Improbable Story of America's Greatest Word* (New York: Oxford University Press, 2010).

23. R. Bailey, "Billions Served: Norman Borlaug Interviewed by Ronald Bailey," *Reason* (April 2000).

24. Ibid.

25. Peter Reuell, "Bringing the Psych Lab Online," *Harvard Gazette* (August 31, 2012). http://news.harvard.edu/gazette/story/2012/08/bringing-the-psych-lab-online/

26. "Gustavo the Great," *60 Minutes*, CBS News (February 11, 2009). http://www.cbsnews.com/2100-18560_162-3841251.html

27. "Dudamel Conducts Mahler 8 — Symphony of a Thousand," Narrated by John Lithgow on LA Phil Live, broadcast by Cineplex to movie theaters, live from Caracas, Venezuela (February 18, 2012).

Chapter Six

1. Tania Singer, Ben Seymour, John O'Doherty, Holger Kaube, Raymond J. Dolan, and Chris D. Frith, "Empathy for Pain Involves the Affective but Not Sensory Components of Pain," *Science* 303, no. 5661 (February 20, 2004): 1157–1162.

2. Tania Singer, Ben Seymour, John P. O'Doherty, Klaas E. Stephan, Raymond J. Dolan, and Chris D. Frith, "Empathic Neural Responses Are Modulated by the Perceived Fairness of Others," *Nature* 439, no. 7075 (January 26, 2006): 466–469.

3. M. Rabin, "Incorporating Fairness into Game Theory and Economics," *The American Economic Review* (1993): 1281–1302.

4. Frans de Waal, *The Age of Empathy: Nature's Lessons for a Kinder Society* (New York: Three Rivers Press, 2010).

5. I. Stewart, *Why Beauty Is Truth: The History of Symmetry* (New York: Basic Books, 2008).

6. S. Williams, *The Moral Premise: Harnessing Virtue & Vice for Box Office Success* (Studio City, CA: Michael Wiese Productions, 2006).

7. E. Fehr and U. Fischbacher, "The Nature of Human Altruism," *Nature* 425, no. 6960 (October 23, 2003): 785–791.

8. P. Zak, *The Moral Molecule* (New York: Dutton Adult, 2012).

9. J. Rayport and B. Jaworski, *Best Face Forward: Why Companies Must Improve Their Service Interfaces with Customers* (Boston: Harvard Business School Press, 2005).

10. Nicola Clark, "Coke Zero Claims Win in Sugar-Free Battles," *Marketing* (August 2, 2006).

11. M. T. Hansen, *Collaboration: How Leaders Avoid the Traps, Create Unity, and Reap Big Results* (Boston: Harvard Business School Press, 2009).

12. Klaus Abbink and Abdolkarim Sadrieh, "The Pleasure of Being Nasty," *Economics Letters* 105, no. 3 (December 2009): 306–308.

13. K. Abbink, D. Masclet, and M. van Veelen, "Reference Point Effects in Antisocial Preferences," CIRANO Working Papers (January 2011).

14. S. Leider, M. Mobius, et al., "What Do We Expect From Our Friends?", Journal of the European Economic Association. Vol. 8, no. 1 (March 2010): 120–138.

15. B. Carey, "The Psychology of Cheating," *The New York Times* (April 16, 2011).

Chapter Seven

1. R. J. Vallerand, C. Blanchard, et al., "Les Passions de l'Ame: On Obsessive and Harmonious Passion," *Journal of Personality and Social Psychology* 85, no. 4 (October 2003): 756–767.

2. B. Rip, S. Fortin, and R. Vallerand, "The Relationship Between Passion and Injury in Dance Students," *Journal of Dance Medicine & Science*, 10, no. 1–2 (June 2006): 14–20.

3. J. Tassel, "Yo-Yo Ma's Journeys," *Harvard Magazine* (March-April, 2000).

4. S. Kaufman, "Increase Your Passion for Work Without Becoming Obsessed," HBR Blog Network (September 21, 2011). http://blogs.hbr.org /cs/2011/09/increase_your_passion_for_work.html

5. "Gabby Sidibe Speaks on Vanity Fair Slight + Serena Williams: Nail Tech," *Global Grind*, Global Grind Staff (February 17, 2010). Retrieved September 21, 2012, from http://globalgrind.com/entertainment/gabby -sidibe-speaks-vanity-fair-slightserena-williams-nail-tech

6. Peter Bodo, "The Real Question Facing Serena Williams," *ESPN Tennis* (January 5, 2012). Retrieved September 21, 2012, from http://espn.go .com/tennis/blog/_/name/bodo_peter/id/7430570/tennis-real-question -facing-serena-williams

7. Chris Chase, "Serena Williams Dominates Maria Sharapova to Cap Career Golden Slam," *Fourth-Place Medal, A Y! Sports Blog* (August 4, 2012). Retrieved September 21, 2012, from http://en-maktoob.news.yahoo.com /blogs/olympics-fourth-place-medal/serena-williams-dominates-maria -sharapova-cap-golden-slam-142852692—oly.html

8. Blake Snyder, "From the Best of Blake's Blogs: 'The Shard of Glass'" (June 22, 2009). Retrieved September 21, 2012, from http://www.blakesnyder .com/2012/04/13/from-the-best-of-blakes-blogs-the-shard-of-glass/

9. "Mandela in His Own Words," *CNN.COM* (June 26, 2008). Retrieved September 21, 2012, from http://edition.cnn.com/2008/WORLD/africa /06/24/mandela.quotes/index.html

10. Robert B. Cialdini, *Influence: The Psychology of Persuasion* (New York: Collins, 1993).

11. L. Festinger, H. W. Riecken, and S. Schachter, *When Prophecy Fails* (New York: Wilder, 2011).

12. "Overwork Blamed in Death of a Top Toyota Engineer," *New York Times*, Business Section (July 10, 2008).

13. O. Segovia, "To Find Happiness Forget About Your Passion," *HBR Blog Network* (January 13, 2012). http://blogs.hbr.org/cs/2012/01/to_find _happiness_forget_about.html

14. Personal interview.

15. Ibid.

Chapter Eight

1. Erving Goffman, *The Presentation of Self in Everyday Life* (Garden City, NJ: Doubleday, 1959).

2. Geoffrey Brewer, "Snakes Top List of Americans' Fears," Gallup News Service (March 19, 2001). Retrieved September 21, 2012, from http://www .gallup.com/poll/1891/snakes-top-list-americans-fears.aspx

3. "This is Your Brain on Jazz: Researchers Use MRI to Study Spontaneity, Creativity," Johns Hopkins Medicine news release (February 2008). http://www.hopkinsmedicine.org/news/media/releases/this_is_your _brain_on_jazz_researchers_use_mri_to_study_spontaneity_creativity

4. Personal interview.

5. D. Davis, M. O'Brien, N. Freemantle, F. M. Wolf, P. Mazmanian, and A. Taylor-Vaisey, "Impact of Formal Continuing Medical Education: Do Conferences, Workshops, Rounds, and Other Traditional Continuing Education Activities Change Physician Behavior or Health Care Outcomes?" *Journal of the American Medical Association* 282, no. 9 (1999): 867–874.

6. Alberto Savoia, *Prototype It* (Seattle: Amazon Digital Services, 2012).

7. Personal interview.

8. N. Morgan, *Trust Me: Four Steps to Authenticity and Charisma* (San Francisco: Jossey-Bass, 2009).

9. "What is NaNoWriMo?" Nanwrimo.org. Retrieved September 21, 2012, from http://www.nanowrimo.org/en/about/whatisnano

10. Taylor Friedman, "How National Novel Writing Month Became a Thing," *SF Weekly* (November 9, 2011). Retrieved September 21, 2012, from http://blogs.sfweekly.com/exhibitionist/2011/11/national_novel_writing _month_n.php

11. "What We're About," The 48 Hour Film Project. Retrieved September 21, 2012, from http://www.48hourfilm.com/en/about/history.php

Chapter Nine

1. David Foster Wallace, "In His Own Words" (September 19, 2008). http://moreintelligentlife.com/story/david-foster-wallace-in-his-own-words

2. Personal interview.

Acknowledgments

Thanks to Quincy's Family Steakhouse; Blockbuster Video; Capitol Newsstand; Agnew, Carter, McCarthy; Erwin-Penland; Furman University; and Duke Corporate Education for teaching me how to work. Thanks to John Fayad for helping me shape some of my earliest thinking that became this book. Thank you, Patricia Snell, my tireless agent, for holding this project to a high standard and ensuring it found a good home. Thank you, Genoveva Llosa, my editor, for teaching me how to write this book. Thank you, Sarah Brown and Sarah Kate Fishback, for your important contributions that saved the day when the day needed saving. Thank you to Duke University's Perkins Library and the world-class research librarians there.

Thank you to my parents for helping me to be confident about my ideas. Thank you to my kids for helping me to be humble about my ideas. *Y gracias Vanessa, por ofrecer la combinación de paciencia, inteligencia, amor y fe que necesité para escribir este libro.*

About the Author

Jake Breeden teaches leaders at some of the world's leading companies. As one of Duke Corporate Education's most active faculty members he has taught in 27 countries, in Asia, Europe, North America, and South America. Some of his clients for leadership development programs include Cisco, Starbucks, Microsoft, Deloitte, HP, Google, and IBM. He has also taught as an adjunct professor for UNC's Kenan-Flagler Business School and conducted training and Webinars for the Association of National Advertiser's (ANA) School of Marketing.

Covering a broad range of topics, Jake has delivered strategy, marketing, communications, and leadership programs. He has developed several original executive education workshops, including "Finding and Tipping Your Organization's Sacred Cows," "Leadership Storytelling Lessons from Hollywood," "The Big Bad Idea Innovation Workshop," and "The Game of Will: A Team-Based Decision-Making Exercise." He has taught at every level in organizations from college hires to board-level executives.

Before starting his own teaching and consulting practice, Jake worked at Duke CE as director of business development and managing director, managing key client relationships and directing business development. He previously served on the faculty and staff at Furman University. As a member of the communication studies faculty at Furman he taught courses in mass communication and advocacy and served as the faculty advisor for the college TV station. As web development director at Furman, he led the development of Engage Furman.com, an award-winning micro-site that pioneered the use of student blogs in 1999. Previously, he started the interactive marketing group for Erwin-Penland, one of the fastest growing ad agencies in the Southeastern United States. He started his career at Agnew, Carter, McCarthy, a PR firm based in Boston.

Jake earned an MBA from Duke University's Fuqua School of Business, an MS in public relations at Boston University's College of Communication, and a BA in English from the University of South Carolina. He lives in Chapel Hill, North Carolina, where his three daughters keep him laughing and learning. More information on Jake is available on his website at www.breedenideas.com.

Index

healthy with, 157–158, 165 buddy system, staying out of trouble with, 158–161, 165 defined, 149 good passion/bad passion, 143–146 job search, passion in, 141–143 leading from behind, 151–152, 164 less obsessive passion, finding, 149–151 looking outside yourself, 161–162, 165 proving yourself right, stopping, 152–154, 164 proving yourself wrong, starting, 154–157, 164 sustaining strength of, 146–149

Hauge, M., 90

HBR Ideacast, 110

Heath Brothers, 87

Heath, C., 86

Heath, D., 86

Hendrickson, T., 189

Henle, M., 7

Hidden beliefs, finding, 11–12

Hoffman, R., 106

Horowitz, A., 108

Human social interaction, metaphor used for (Goffman), 169

Hunkering down, 63–65, 68 and success, 6

I

IBM, 179–180

Ichino, A., 30

Ideas, curating, 90–93

Imbalance, embracing, 44–45

Improv comedy: cardinal rule of, 173 game, 174 and preparation, 173–174

In Search of Excellence (Peters/Waterman), 97–98

Indecision to act, 38–39

Influence: The Psychology of Persuasion (Cialdini), 155

Innovator's Dilemma, The (Christensen), 5–6

Intensity, practicing with, 180–182, 186

Internal drives, and fairness, 7–8

iPhone (Apple), 75

J

Jablonski, D., 6

Jacobs, J., 99

Jacobson, D., 108

Jaworski, B., 129

Jazz pianist study (John Hopkins), 172

Jealousy, 9

Jiro Dreams of Sushi (documentary), 183

Job search, passion in, 141–143

Johns Hopkins Medicine news release, 172

Johnson, J., 51

Joy of Destruction (game), 133

Juillerat, T. L., 16

Just Do It slogan (Nike), 154

K

Kaplan, R., 28

Karoshi, 157

Kaube, H., 120

Kaufman, C., 87

Kaufman, S. B., 74, 146

Kelly, K., 86

Kennedy, J., 31

Kethley, B., 21

Kill Bill, 39

Kim, S. H., 76

King, S., 78, 83

Kirchner, L., 147

Klein, H., 19

Kodak, 76

Kounin, J., 7

Koystra, E., 158–159

Koystra, F., 158–159

Koystra, M., 159

Kramer, J., 96

Kramer, S., 36

L

Laliberte, M.L.N., 4

Laporte, N., 104

Lasseter, J., 100

Lazardis, M., 49–50